A Parliament of Souls

A Parliament of Souls

LIMITS AND RENEWALS 2

Stephen R. L. Clark

CLARENDON PRESS · OXFORD

1990

Oxford University Press, Walton Street, Oxford OX2 6DP
Oxford New York Toronto
Delhi Bombay Calcutta Madras Karachi
Petaling Jaya Singapore Hong Kong Tokyo
Nairobi Dar es Salaam Cape Town
Melbourne Auckland
and associated companies in
Berlin Ibadan

Oxford is a trade mark of Oxford University Press

Published in the United States by
Oxford University Press, (USA)

© *Stephen R.L. Clark 1990*

British Library Cataloguing in Publication Data
Clark, Stephen R. L. (Stephen Richard Lyster)
A parliament of souls: limits and renewals 2.
1. Man. Soul: Philosophical perspectives
I. Title
128.1
ISBN 0–19–824236–0

Library of Congress Cataloging in Publication Data
Clark, Stephen R. L.
A parliament of souls/Stephen R. L. Clark.
p. cm.—(Limits and renewals; 2)
Includes bibliographical references.
1. Religion—Philosophy. 2. Philosophy of mind. 3. Soul.
4. Neoplatonism. I. Title. II. Series: Clark, Stephen R. L.
Limits and renewals; 2. BL51.C548 1990 90–33120
ISBN 0–19–824236–0

Typeset by Cambrian Typesetters, Frimley, Surrey
Printed and bound in
Great Britain by Bookcraft (Bath) Ltd,
Midsomer Norton, Avon

Acknowledgements

W. H. Auden's poem, 'The Shield of Achilles' is quoted from Auden's *Collected Poems* by permission of Faber and Faber, and of Random House.

Robert Graves's poem 'Outlaws' is quoted from *Collected Poems 1975*, by permission of A. P. Watt Limited and Oxford University Press, New York on behalf of the executors and the Estate of Robert Owen.

Ursula Leguin's verse is quoted from *The Wizard of Earthsea* by permission of Houghton Mifflin Co., Boston, Mass.

Kathleen Raine's poem 'Message from Home' is quoted from *Selected Poems* 1988 (Golgonooza Press) by permission of Kathleen Raine.

The works of Olaf Stapledon are quoted with the permission of John D. Stapledon and Mary (Stapledon) Shenai.

W. B. Yeats's poem 'Two Songs from a Play' is quoted from the *Collected Poems of W. B. Yeats* (copyright 1928 by Macmillan, renewed 1956 by Georgie Yeats) by permission of A. P. Watt Ltd, on behalf of Michael B. Yeats and Macmillan London Ltd., and of Macmillan, New York.

Preface

This second volume of *Limits and Renewals* is based on the Stanton lectures in the Philosophy of Religion given in Cambridge in the autumn of 1987. All those I thanked in the preface to the first volume, *Civil Peace and Sacred Order*, continue to merit my gratitude, especially Nicholas Lash, Stephen Sykes, and Dorothy Emmet. Some of the material presented here has also been tried out in Aberystwyth, Belfast, Glasgow, Boulder and Liverpool. The Stapledon Collection housed in Liverpool University Library was well served by Michael Perkin till his early retirement: my thanks to him, to the Stapledon family, and to Robert Crossley for making this resource available.

The final version of this volume was prepared during a term as visiting professor at Vanderbilt University in Nashville, and I am especially grateful to my colleagues and students there for showing me that I was not quite as freakish as I have sometimes been encouraged to suppose! John Compton, Idit Dobbs-Weinstein, Clement Dore, Jean Elshtain, John Lachs, John Post, Charles Scott, and Don Sherburne have all helped me to understand my own arguments, in this and the following volume. Reading Plotinus with a group of enthusiastic graduate students was a revelation. It is also appropriate to add that this term was a welcome relief from the seemingly unending task of justifying one's own, and one's department's, existence by the writing of research-reports, the filling-in of forms, and the lobbying of influential persons. So much time is spent on these matters in the contemporary British university as to leave one very doubtful what it is that is being justified.

The epigraph from Chesterton was drawn to my attention by Borges, who cites this same passage three times in *Other Inquisitions* (1964: 50, 104, 155). It serves as a reminder that I see no good reason to restrict my reading to those few thinkers that have, for whatever reason, achieved canonical status. And also as a reminder that it is possible to argue clearly and cogently without abandoning all the literary graces. I make no claim to write as well as Chesterton or Borges: I could hardly help writing better than some present-day philosophers. The literary graces can conceal vapidity of thought, but so can the sort of writing all too familiar in both the analytical and the hermeneutical schools. If I have managed to avoid some of those failings, a large part of the credit must go to Gillian Clark, my best friend and severest critic. Where I have failed to avoid them, let the reader beware.

S.R.L.C.

26 April 1989

Contents

Man knows that there are in the soul tints more bewildering, more numberless, and more nameless than the colours of an autumn forest. . . . Yet he seriously believes that these things can every one of them, in all their tones and semi-tones, in all their blends and unions, be accurately represented by an arbitrary system of grunts and squeals. He believes that an ordinary civilized stockbroker can really produce out of his own inside noises which denote all the mysteries of memory and all the agonies of desire. (Chesterton, 1904)

I

Individuals and Persons

Abstract Argument and Partial Judgement

One of the most endearing philosophical models of this century has been that propounded by John Rawls, of abstract individuals working out, behind a veil of ignorance, what laws they should accept or decree for themselves to live under, once the veil is withdrawn and they discover what it is that they admire or desire, and what their socio-economic status is to be. My principal criticism of this model, as it is also my principal criticism of utilitarian theory, is that no such debate is strictly conceivable. Once put us behind such a veil and we can have no idea at all what we would prefer to do or have done. There is no value-neutral body of law, and no real human persons not embedded in particular historical and personal circumstances. There are no abstract individuals, and Justice cannot be what such abstract, ahistorical individuals would decide upon (if they existed), because such beings could not decide on anything at all. The argument goes back at least to Louis de Bonald (see Holmes 1984: 222 f.).

In my first volume I was constantly proposing that we are bound to work within a 'conservative' rather than a 'liberal' framework, even if such workings and reworkings do often issue in 'liberal' action. Indeed my object was to suggest that if we want liberal action at all, we have to rely upon conservative thought: liberal or enlightenment method cannot, when honestly applied, give us the results that good liberal souls imagine that they want. Free thought, moral relativism, 'scientific' theorizing and the rest of the modernist armoury are inadequate to defend the liberal advantages of a free society that modernists imagine they have wrested from the old regime. Bonald's argument, of course, was directed against liberal action, his rejection of liberal individualism an attempted defence of hierarchical society. That is not my motive (though I do not think it *obvious* that all hierarchy is evil), any more than I have any wish to advocate a Marxist dictatorship of the proletariat or—more probably—of the party. That latter point is worth emphasizing now because one of my most baffled memories is of delivering a paper to a meeting of the Society for the Study of Theology (since anthologized as 'Gaia and the Forms of Life': Clark 1983) which was promptly, and indefeasibly, characterized as crypto-Marxist by a West Indian bishop. What I had said then, and have now repeated, was that there are no such things as individuals, to be divorced from the social and physical setting within which we have our being. I remain baffled that anyone should suppose that the only way of avoiding Marxism (or in times past the Bourbons) is to believe in the existence of abstract individuals. The institutions of a free society, which I wholeheartedly support, are best served by acknowledging what we really are: nodes on a web, elements of a wider whole, creatures utterly dependent for their lives and minds and welfare on the communities of which knowingly or unknowingly they are a part. 'The patriot', so Berkeley said, 'aims at his private good in the public. The knave makes the public subservient to his private interest. The former considers himself as part of a whole, the latter considers himself as the whole' (1948: vi. 254). We defend a free society best when we stop pretending that every rational creature would agree to live in such a free society whatever her personal virtues and code of values, just as we defend the values of science and scholarship best when we stop imagining that they can be deduced from value-free truisms. A genuine society of strangers would not be a free society, or even much of a society. Our freedom, so far as it exists, rests upon shared values and beliefs as obviously and as unavoidably as any past hierarchical or caste society. 'In a caste ridden, sect-torn and regionally compartmentalized society atomism fosters nation building and even democratization' (Holmes 1984: 224): but such atomism is itself a social form, a truth 'by convention' and not 'by nature' (which is not to say that it is false or unreal).

Political philosophy is not my principal concern in this volume. But it must inevitably be a part of my concern:

although I shall be discussing a variety of issues in the philosophy of mind, it is precisely the point I have just been making that we cannot sensibly ask what abstract minds or persons or souls are like. The personal beings we seek to understand, ourselves, are concrete, politically structured beings. Man is a political animal in a very powerful sense. That this is a Marxist point, and a Bonaldian, in no way shows that I am a crypto-Marxist, or a crypto-fascist, any more than (and perhaps somewhat less than) MacIntyre.

Consider Hume's enormously persuasive rhetoric, and note with MacIntyre that

his final court of appeal can be no more than the appeal to the passions of men of good sense, to a concurrence of feelings among the worldly. . . . The passions of some are to be preferred to the passions of others. Whose preferences reign? The preferences of those who accept the stability of property, of those who understand chastity in women as a virtue only because it is a useful device to ensure that property is passed only to legitimate heirs, of those who believe that the passage of time confers legitimacy upon what was originally acquired by violence and aggression. What Hume identifies as the standpoint of universal human nature turns out in fact to be that of the prejudices of the Hanoverian ruling elite. Hume's moral philosophy presupposes allegiance to a particular kind of social structure as much as Aristotle's does. (MacIntyre 1981: 215)

If abstract values are given enough content to make any significant difference, their content is—to put it mildly—likely to be determined by the attitudes and *Weltanschauung* of the dominant group. Because we pretend, even to ourselves, that the laws of the land are those that any rational being would prescribe, that they depend not at all on particular evaluations, we may be the more shameless in imposing our ideals on others. If, on the other hand, we seriously acknowledge that talk of Justice or Happiness 'in the abstract' is so vague as to be effectively meaningless, such values cannot serve to settle any point between bourgeois liberal, Muslim, Marxist, nationalist, animal liberationist, or mainstream Christian. 'For quite non-Marxist reasons Marx was in the right when he argued against the English trade-unionists of the 1860s that appeals to Justice were pointless, since there are rival conceptions of justice formed by and informing the life of rival groups' (MacIntyre 1981: 215).[1]

A meeting of minds and manners here is not impossible, but there is little reason to expect that calculations of 'total happiness' (i.e. counting how many, and how strong, the preferences that are satisfied), 'abstract justice', or the 'natural rights' of beings that are, irrespective of their social setting, self-owners or subjects of a life (see Clark 1987), will settle the point between them. 'To live honestly'—but what duties and privileges are they that constitute the particular being of each honest life? 'To injure none'—but what counts as injury, and who as a creature that must not be injured? 'To each his own'—but what is one's own, and who or what is to count as owner? Those Europeans who imagined that they had 'bought' land or labour or security from an Amerindian 'chief' were, in their terms, justly incensed to find that the land would not stay bought. Amerindians, in their terms, were as justly outraged by the greed and superstition of the Europeans. How could they possibly suppose that the land itself could be given away forever, that they had been granted anything more than a permission to share its fruits with all its other inhabitants? 'Justice', in historical fact, has been the name given to the interest of the stronger, and the efforts of political philosophers to ground a particular dispensation in abstract or universal right are as empty as the parallel efforts of epistemologists to derive our ordinary, traditionally grounded and socially mediated 'knowledge' from axioms that just any rational being would be bound to accept. 'Adolf Eichmann insisted at his trial that he had always acted according to Kant's imperative. He clearly envisioned the extermination of the Jewish people as a universal law to be universally followed' (Pannenberg 1969: 104).

Must this account involve the rejection of impartiality as a value? That may certainly seem to be the implication. Spokesmen for a culture and tradition not well represented in the ruling élite may be equally resentful of those who pretend to judge them 'impartially', but who entertain no doubts about the whole *Gestalt* within which they work.

[1] Some of what follows is given a somewhat different context (and direction) in Clark 1988*a*.

Everyone thinks himself free of prejudice because no one is able impartially to examine himself. . . . One can see the place one stands only by moving to another, at which point a different place is concealed. (Martin 1981: 66)

'Impartiality' is either a cloak for unconscious prejudice or a condition in which no decisions can any longer be taken: one cannot be impartial, for example, between the claims of Western liberal individualism and Muslim fundamentalism when the duties and privileges of a young girl are in question—unless by speaking from within some other equally intransigent tradition. There are self-styled liberals, of course, who feebly suggest that it is merely cultural or racial prejudice that leads us to disapprove of clitoridectomy, the veil, and childhood betrothal ceremonies. It was 'wrong', no doubt, of British officials to seek to suppress thuggery, or suttee, or caste discrimination: wrong to do so because these practices were part of a distinctive 'culture', even though it was equally 'part of a distinctive culture' that the British seek to suppress them. This is no more sensible than inverted snobbery. The decision to provide *hallal* meats to Muslim schoolchildren in state-run schools is not an 'impartial' one: it is, precisely, a decision to be partial to the claims of one sect as against another. Those who praise that decision as 'anti-racist' are usually quite blind to the moral objections raised by animal welfarists.

Can we really abandon all the duties of practical judgement? Can we really hesitate to call child sacrifice 'murder' merely because those who perform the sacrifice think differently about the act? Was the Holocaust really 'just the accepted Nazi way of doing things'? It is easy to reply that such practices rest upon ontological assumptions that are merely false, that the Nazi category of the subhuman is empty, that we are all of 'one kind' with those whom liberal practice would wish to protect, all actually or potentially autonomous individuals who can only be held responsible for 'their own' actions, and not for those of their race. But this reply, however well-meaning, cannot be sustained if at the same time we acknowledge that who and what 'we' are is a socio-cultural formation. There is no abstract 'fact of the matter' discernible by all parties, and no genuinely world-neutral body of methodological principles, with which Nazi, Carthaginian, Aztec, or even medieval European purposes could be held, somehow, compatible.

We live and act and have our beings in established crafts and communities. There is nothing humanly recognizable that human individuals *would* be like if they had not grown up in a community, and we cannot sensibly ask ourselves what wholly deracinated, solitary, uninformed 'intelligences' would agree on if they had to, nor what measures they would take to achieve a natural happiness.

Allegiances such as [those to family or community or people, as bearers of this history, as sons and daughters of this revolution, as citizens of this republic] are more than values I happen to have or aims I espouse at any given time. To imagine a person incapable of constitutive attachments such as these is not to conceive an ideally free and rational agent, but to imagine a person wholly without character, without moral depth. (Sandel 1982: 179)

What constitutes happiness for any of us is partly determined by our view of life, the universe, and everything. What identifies a creature as one with which we must achieve some workable relationship is our traditional stack of stereotypes and working practices. Hunter-gatherers, pastoralists, and traditional agriculturalists must reckon themselves members, at some workable level, of a community of gods, the dead, the living and the unborn, animals and crops, and the historically patterned land. Antigone, in Sophocles' play, did not oppose Creon in order to stand out as an individual, nor yet to achieve some goal of greater 'happiness' for all: she buried her brother because she thought of herself as a member of that family, with established duties that could not be abrogated by despotic command. Rationalizing moralists in the Declining West may reckon such things superstitious, not such as rational intelligences would agree to 'in the abstract'. How could Antigone's brother, or his corpse, have any 'right' to be buried? But there could be no rational intelligences in the abstract, and therefore no supracultural, unhistorical agreements of the kind lauded by Rousseau and his successors, nor any non-moral account of 'happiness' such that moral rules could be seen as merely technical advice on how to get 'it'.

Once rationalizing moralism and its attendant mythology

of 'pure intelligences behind a veil of ignorance' or pure Benthamite hedonists have been dismissed, it seems that we are condemned to the life of more or less fervent partisans, that we have no recourse but to the 'good faith' and 'traditionally grounded intelligence' of persons reared in class, sect, craft, party, and historic nation. The claims of justice and utility alike have usually been considered in a non-historical context, with the unspoken assumption that historical rights and traditionally assessed utilities are not the province of moral minds, or of philosophers. But, as Berkeley pointed out, 'though we should grant that (a prince) had originally no right to the crown, yet when (he) is once in possession of it and you have sworn allegiance to him you are no longer at liberty to inquire by what unrighteous steps he might have obtained it' (1948: vi. 57). Once the anti-historical assumption is displaced, must we accept that civil peace is only a temporary expedient, that there can be no appeal to any wider loyalties or goods than those embedded in partisan tradition?

Thus: Albert, an honest mink-farmer, believes himself entitled under the law to keep and slaughter minks, while Belle, a radical zoophile, believes herself entitled to rescue her imprisoned kin, wrongfully enslaved. British law, being what it is, is not impartial in this matter; it is, in effect, Albert's Law. Belle may agree that it is better than it would be if it were Cuthbert's—Cuthbert being an honest organizer of dogfights and badger-baiting expeditions—or Drogo's—Drogo being a stereotypically humourless fanatic who would rather organize ritual murders. All sides *may* agree (but some obviously do not) that they would rather not force each other into open war, knowing what that condition is like. But the laws under which they do in fact live are certainly not those minimal laws that they might adopt to avoid Hobbes's state of nature. Nor are they those more extensive laws that they or their representatives might, under certain historical conditions, come to acknowledge as authoritative. The High Courts of Parliament are no longer, if ever they were, the place where divergent crafts, communities, and traditions came together to develop a new moral consensus for the larger community they ruled. 'Loyalty to my country, to my community—which remains unalterably a central virtue—becomes detached from

obedience to the government which happens to rule me'
(MacIntyre 1981: 236 f.).

Respect for individual liberties under the rule of law is not
the product of abstract argument (for no such arguments
work), but of a historically grounded sense of mutual respect
for fellow inhabitants of these offshore islands. What happens
when those inhabitants and temporary sojourners no longer
share enough of their attitudes and moral categories to
support a willing obedience to the Queen in Parliament, when
the Law is (plausibly) dismissed as 'Tory Law' or 'Militant
Takeover'? Kipling's insight that

> If you cross over the sea,
> instead of over the way,
> you may end by (think of it!) looking on We
> as only a sort of They

(Kipling 1927: 710)

has been used to lend emotional, though hardly rational,
support for the idea that all possible life-styles and world-
views *ought* to be given equal respect—which amounts to
Plato's disparaging description of the 'democratic' principle
(*Republic* 8, 557)! The Pauline respect for individual conscience
had rested on the conviction that God might demand from one
what He refused to another, that no one of us had a right to
dictate to her fellow servants merely because their instructions
seemed to her weak intellect to be at odds with hers. 'No one is
entitled to outdo the conscience of somebody else by his own
superior knowledge; no individual conscience can be silenced
simply by instruction from those wiser' (Dihle 1982: 81, after
St Paul). But that doctrine of course precisely defines one life-
style and world-view as better deserving of respect than
certain imaginable and all-too-real others. Tyranny is wrong
because something else is right. And Paul certainly did not
suppose that just any life could be adopted 'in good
conscience': someone who pleads that he is 'conscience-
bound' to beat children to death or betray his neighbours to
the Gestapo is defying what has been unequivocally revealed
to the abiding tradition within which our talk of conscience
makes sense. Once that standpoint is abandoned, we end with
the irredeemably fatuous remark attributed to a teacher

recently: 'I do not mind what a child believes when he leaves school, as long as he believes it by being true to himself' (*The Times*, 25 March 1987). Or in other words, 'Yes, I know he sells heroin, beats his common-law wife, rapes children, tortures cats for fun and profit, betrays his country and cheats at cards, but he's very sincere.' The notion that 'being true to oneself' is one's only real duty at least had some content in Polonius' day, for 'the Self' involved was that true self, 'abiding within the senses, a person who consists of understanding, a light within the heart' (*Brhadaranyaka Upanishad* 4. 3. 7). Obedience to conscience was not the same as doing what one happened to feel like. Those modern liberals who imagine themselves illogically obligated to respect every individual's whim, and at the same time lack any coherent concept of what is to count as an individual, are at the mercy of any other imaginable system of identification, any other whim or prejudice. To resent tyranny is itself a choice, a value-judgement, an essentially contestable identification. Giving a young girl the choice whether to be a loyal Muslim daughter or an independent citizen is itself to identify her as the latter, whose decision about 'her' life must be respected. And even the limits of what such a citizen's life may be are, obviously, contestable: is an unborn child subsumed into its mother's life?

It is worth remarking in this context that far too many people have drawn the wrong lesson from J. P. Sartre's little story of the young man faced by a choice between looking after his mother and joining the Free French (a story that has long since escaped from its original Sartrean provenance). It may be true that there is no rule to say which he should do; it may even be true that the young man, in seeking Sartre's advice, had already chosen what sort of advice he wished to hear. But why should it follow that any and every choice between alternative courses of action must be as unprincipled, as 'up to us'? Consider the town elders who asked Delphic Apollo whether they might surrender suppliants to the enemy. Apollo replied that they could. One of the elders, dissatisfied with the answer, began dislodging the swallows' nests from the temple eaves. Apollo spoke from the sanctuary to demand an explanation, and on being reminded that he had himself advised the elders to betray their suppliants, replied that he had done so that the elders might learn from bitter experience what happened to people who practised such betrayals.

Have we no recourse, as MacIntyre seems to suggest, but to cultivate our parties till one of them informs the world-consciousness of a new civil community? 'What matters at this stage is the construction of local forms of community within which civility and the intellectual and moral life can be sustained through the new dark ages which are already upon us. . . . We are waiting not for a Godot, but for another—doubtless very different—St Benedict' (MacIntyre 1981: 245). But MacIntyre is perhaps exaggerating our problem. The rationalist implicitly assumes

   (i) that we can distinguish between 'natural' and 'conventional' morality;
  (ii) that this distinction will be Newtonian in character, between what 'we' would decide 'ideally' and what we decide when influenced by historical accident;
 (iii) that we need the distinction if we are to be able to criticize the conventions of our or any other day;
 (iv) that such a natural morality will consist of an axiomatizable set of rules.

Once doubt is cast on the second and fourth assumptions, it may seem that the first will also fail, for how else than by abstract rationality could we hope to identify a morality that is more than conventional? If the third remains unchallenged, it must seem that we can only challenge one party's views and actions by appealing to another's, that all moral reflection is incurably partisan, and a genuinely *rational* critique is impossible. 'The ascendancy of faith may be impractical, but the reign of knowledge is incomprehensible. The problem for statesmen of this age is how to educate the masses, and literature and science cannot give the solution' (Newman 1979: 88). On these terms the new St Benedict will be one more cult-leader, and those faced by that prospect may decide that a decaying individualism, with all its faults, is preferable. MacIntyre's promised statement of his 'systematic account of [moral] rationality' (1981: 242) may provide a non-partisan justification for his preferred 'Benedictines'. As I have not so far read his most recent work, *Whose Justice? Which Rationality*, I offer the following sketch in ignorance of what that systematic account may be.

Our problem is that we seem to be faced by two alternatives: either we must be able to identify a Newtonian or Archimedean point from which all parties can be judged, or else we are thrown back upon the mere confrontation of ideas and ideals, to be settled by war or by such quieter versions of military confrontation as go under the guise of modern politics. This problem in turn has two dimensions to it. On the one hand, we have the practical, political problem of securing as much of our own way with the world as we can in the absence of an absolute theocracy or world-emperor with clearly established priorities and laws. This is not an abstract question, nor one about the negotiations of abstract intelligences: it is an issue in present-day, power politics, a question of how much I and my friends and well-wishers can secure at the cost of how few concessions to those who might be our allies on particular occasions and our enemies on others. There can be no one rationally discernible answer to this problem, especially as all proposed solutions will subtly alter the balance of power even as they record one particular moment of its swing. Nor do all parties to such negotiations have a common perspective on what they stand to gain: those who do not suppose that the Nature of Things is on their side will be willing enough to claim what minor gains they can; those who expect their side to win outright need not bargain away their futures for a short-term gain. How exactly can liberal politicians reach agreements with those they reckon 'fanatics'? Even the assumption that we have no absolute theocrat or world-emperor is in practice moot: modernists, of almost every theological description, assume that God is an absentee landlord, not even to be expected back. If they are wrong, then the Day will vindicate the righteous—and those who expect such vindication would be fools to abandon God's kingdom for any partial short-term gain.

The second dimension of our problem may be more accessible to philosophical injury: can we identify a non-partisan rationality without recourse to Archimedean points? If there are no abstract individuals, and no moral or metaphysical propositions that can be demonstrated to just anyone if they are 'honest and unprejudiced enough' (unless such honesty amounts to a particular sort of virtue defined by a concrete community), we cannot distinguish between 'truths by nature' and 'truths by convention' as if that distinction was the same as that between 'rationally systematized truths' and 'mere prejudices or theory-laden observations'. But it does not follow that it is irrational to depend upon the mass of received opinion in a free society with deep historical roots: in the absence of an inner light that uniquely and unprecedentedly acquaints us with things as they are, we have to rely in matters moral and matters scientific on rational consensus. We cannot reconstruct that consensus from indefeasible axioms evident to any imaginable intelligence, and the policy of subverting existing norms by demanding that degree of confirmation is, as Berkeley said, 'our present impending danger, . . . the setting up of private judgement or an inward light in opposition to human and divine laws. Such an inward conceited principle always at work and proceeding gradually and steadily, may be sufficient to dissolve any human fabric of polity or civil government' (1948 vi. 217). It does not follow that no rational criticism of an existing polity is possible, any more than the physical sciences are incorrigible merely because there is no known and incontrovertible theory from which their progress can be judged. I should add, in anticipation of a later volume, that it is wholly irrational to speak of scientific progress while at the same time we disdain all knowledge of realistic truth.

Social Relativism Revisited

To recapitulate: the persons we are, and whom we encounter, are inescapably historical and social beings, who make their decisions on the basis of beliefs and preferences and metaphysical commitments that we cannot justify by strict deduction from logically undeniable first principles. To replace the existing body of information and practice by some arbitrary other would be at least as absurd. Where criticisms of an existing body do arise it is not unreasonable to suspect that they serve the class interests or express the hopes and prejudices of a subculture within the larger community. 'We' is a term that refers to a class of entities relevantly similar under some description to the presumed speaker and her preferred hearers. Some such communities, including our own, are so far flexible as to allow or even encourage an imaginative attention to other *Gestalten,* other ways of speaking and classifying.[2] The eventual choice between such *Gestalten* as are live options for 'us' cannot be Cartesian, but it does not follow that it must therefore be sheerly voluntarist, as if logical demonstration and arbitrary whim were exhaustive alternatives. Our real assent is a response to a concrete, lived reality, not the conclusion of a demonstrative argument nor a gambler's hypothesis.

So what are we, or what might 'we' agree to be, if we are not deracinated, abstract intelligences? My answer is probably already obvious, though it will take me a volume to spell it out in detail. I believe us to be just what I have already described, namely finite, shifting, and radically dependent modes of a physical, social, and spiritual universe that is not now coherently systematizable by us, but which has a higher rationality of its own. So far, indeed, all that I have said could be taken as a common modern theme, even if it is one that has not sufficiently affected moral and political philosophy, and even if modernists have failed to register that one central theme of religious practice the world over is just the attempt to awaken in us an abiding sense of that dependency. Before going any further I must disengage my exposition from other, more relativistic or consciously reductionist ones.

This being here, this person, is inextricably and essentially a male intellectual of the twentieth-century liberal West, who speaks of himself, who 'creates himself' by his speaking, with the linguistic tools provided by Western history, through those languages that I shall collectively call 'Westron'. 'I' here-now names a speaker, a psycho-physical organism that is

---

[2] It is worth pointing out that despite the enormous crimes and follies of Western Civilization it is at once the oldest continuous human tradition, and the most interested in other human traditions. The two properties are not accidentally conjoined.

variously responsible for a range of past events and future expectations, that is recognizably and determinedly 'the same' under various possible disguises and changed circumstances, that could have done all sorts of things it has not done, and that can be judged under the same laws as any other speaker. 'The human being, as a person, is a complex of social relationships' (Radcliffe-Brown 1940: 193). This person here, 'I', is a social construct, and probably a rather more complex one than standard accounts of 'personal identity' allow, just as there are many more 'finite provinces of meaning' than rationalists have acknowledged. My suspicion is—one that I shall spell out in more detail in later chapters—that ancient concepts (as 'we' say) of 'the soul'—were no more confused or contradictory than ours. 'I' here-now names a bundle of threads reaching back towards a birth and forward to some death or other. How far the threads are judged to stretch, how tightly they are bound, how easily they may be distinguished from 'other' bundles past and present, are matters of socio-political and metaphysical judgement. People from a different nexus would speak and behave differently and judge different things 'the same'. Even what is meant by 'people' and its cognate terms must vary between traditions: in ours here-now a person is an identifiable animal organism having moral ties over time with particular 'person-stages' and with particular significant others. There are or may be other traditions whose bearers 'we' would regard as fragments or communities or mere appendages. And, of course, contrariwise.

From all this some have inferred that we are confronted by so radically incommensurable a set of traditions that the bilingual constitute a walking miracle. It has been suggested that as the Japanese language lacks any single locution to refer to the speaker, whoever or whatever she may be, at whatever time of life or in whatever context of social obligation, the Japanese speaker (as 'we' would identify her) can have no concept of her self, and cannot be 'a self' in the way that speakers of Westron would expect. That bilingual Japanese do not report that their selves flip in and out of existence as they switch their language is only because there is no language in which they could report so bizarre an event, even to themselves. In Westron, so to speak, they are recognizably

and indefeasibly personal selves of the same kind as the rest of
us; in Japanese they are not—or rather there is no 'they' as a
single class at all, and no one identity that is, linguistically,
the subject of all the experiences that would, in Westron, be
attributed to 'I', 'he', 'she'. That our languages, or at any rate
our languages and social practices together, thus determine
the nature of our possible experience, 'the limits of our
worlds', is a surprisingly attractive thought. What could our
having such and such a concept be except being prepared to
speak in certain ways, to countenance certain practical
implications, to direct our minds in one way and not another?
If those ways and means are never strictly demonstrable from
what would be self-evident principle no matter to whom the
evidence was offered, can we speak of how 'the world' is apart
from the structures 'we' develop? If the Kwakiutl have a
different name for every stage of life, as Mauss reported
(Mauss 1985: 9), have they any way of saying, or thinking,
who it is that passes through those stages?

  Harré, who has endorsed such thoughts as these (see 1984:
97), is perhaps less constrained by anti-realist arguments[3]
than some: he is, as I am, conscious of the mass of other
creatures in the world and confident that at least some of the
concepts we develop for our own purposes must apply to the
non-human too. 'Conventional' and 'natural' truth are subtly
intermingled. Not all truths are of our making, nor all
conventions either. What counts as 'of the same species' is, in
part, a matter determined by our language (so that, in a sense,
whales are indubitably fish); but there are real species out
there in the world, determined by the preferences of the non-
human. Fido is a dog if he is recognized as such by other dogs,
and humble scientific realists aim to edge their language into a
sort of correspondence with the language that the world
speaks to itself. We must, as Aristotle said (*Metaphysics* 1, 984ª
18, ᵇ10), allow the truth to lead us. In corrected Westron
whales are not fish. Such a hope, of cutting at the world's

---

[3] That is to say, by the insistence that 'being true' or 'being real' is only
and entirely a function of what 'we' seriously say, that there is nothing
'outside the text'. I hope it is not necessary to point out that I regard this
notion, whether in Anglo-Saxon or in French philosophy, as both morally
and epistemologically outrageous.

joints (as Plato puts it), must make it clear that even if our language and social practice does limit what we can think, not all languages are therefore equal. If it is the case that Japanese speakers do not, in Japanese, allow for self-identity of a kind that 'we' would recognize, it does not follow that the Japanese are not of one and the same kind as us, any more than Nazis were of a different species from Jews or Gypsies just because they said they were.

But though there is, I think, an underlying realism in Harré's work, he does say some things that suggest that he would class most of our folk-psychology (as well as that of the Japanese) as merely ideal, 'true' only in inverted commas, and having no sound explanatory function in any realistic metaphysic. I recognize a class of truths that are *made* true, 'true by convention', but are now really true, and have real effects. Those with anti-realist sympathies suppose that such 'truths' are not 'really true' at all, either because there is nothing at all 'outside the text', or because what is outside is of a radically different kind from anything 'we' easily recognize. I retain the older vision, that there is a real world which can yet enter in to our conscious experience: *nous*, which is the intelligible universe, comes 'from outside' into the inquiring mind. The question is, for me as well as for Harré, do the identities we here-now recognize have any real, abiding status in the world of truth? Nothing that is 'really' true here-now—so some may think—is true because there are as a matter of non-ideal fact certain particular identities. In giving the lectures from which this book derives I remarked that 'we add nothing to an explanation of why this body here is uttering these English words by referring to a real identity of the speaker with the one or several writers that was or were composing them a month or two ago'. It was quite enough to point to the causal connections, neurological and otherwise, that link that far away event with that here-now. The point is 'now' more obvious: what does it matter if anyone 'now' (as you, my reader, see it) is 'identical' with that far composer? Even if (as is very likely) intentional explanation cannot be identified with any such neurological causality but is still real (not merely ideal), it is still not clear that my self-identity is needed to provide a hermeneutical account of what is 'meant'. There

are plenty of Buddhist schools, after all, where no such self is
to be believed, where there is no 'fact of the matter' to end
such questionings as 'how many real subjects are there here?'
Are there any? And if there is no real truth here, but only
several ideal constructions, we may acknowledge that a quasi-
Japanese diversity expresses even 'our' experience better.

For Harré, in setting up a contrast between the Japanese
and Westron modes, falls victim to a tendency that I shall
have many occasions to notice. What he is contrasting is not
how Westron speakers speak and think in every circumstance
of our confusing lives with what Japanese speakers similarly
do, but rather what some Westron thinkers have supposed we
ought to say with what the mass of Japanese speakers
observably do say. Just so Dihle, for example, contrasts the
alleged absence of any concept of 'the will' in ancient Greek
with its alleged presence in modern Westron as evidenced by
the thought of Kant: 'Kant's remark about good will as the
only factor in human life which is unconditionally praiseworthy
makes no sense whatever in Greek ethical thought' (Dihle
1982: 37)—but whoever said it made much sense in modern
Westron thought?[4] Similarly, it may be true that the Japanese
language provides a wealth of pronouns and modifiers to
express the particular moment and social relations of the
speakers concerned, while lacking any single word to capture
the unity through time of something that can take many social
roles, or the difference at a time between one individual of a
kind and another. But Westron allows us many shifts of style
and accent and mannerism, depending on the moment and
the social relations of the speakers, to the point that we could
quite intelligibly say that we are not the 'same persons' when
we speak as lovers, parents, teachers, employers, citizens, or
officials, or when we speak to one above or below us in the
unofficial but very powerful social ranking. We can be glad, as
I am, that we do not inhabit the sort of caste society against
which early Buddhists rebelled (and how could they have

---

[4] Or consider Harré's observations on Kwakiutl aesthetic theory, that
the artist is releasing a real being from the surrounding stone: how different
from 'our' view of things (Harré 1984: 88)! But just the same theory is
attested by the authors of the *Philokalia*, and by ps-Dionysius (1971: 194 f.),
who are certainly not marginal to our real history.

done, if it were really true that 'we' can never think of
ourselves save in the terms allowed 'us' by our native
tongues?). But it would be foolish to suppose that there are no
analogies at all between even the most liberal and would-be
'class-less' society and those hierarchical societies that have
dominated the human universe for millenia. Conversely, it is
simply unbelievable, to me, that the author, say of *The Tale of
Genji*, was speaking of an utterly alien society in which Jane
Austen would have been entirely at a loss. The Lady
Murasaki was as aware as any Westron novelist that her
fellows were at once engagingly different and inescapably the
same, and herself records that her father used to sigh and say
to her (apropos of her quickness in learning Chinese), 'If only
you were a boy how proud and happy I would be'. In other
words people were well able to envisage there being something
which was in fact a young girl but might have been a boy and
future court official, even though Chinese was apparently
considered beyond the normal power of women or the
proprieties (Waley 1935: vii f.). Like Mauss, whose observations are so often appealed to in defence of radical idealism, I
simply do not believe that there has ever been a human being
unaware of her own individuality (Mauss 1985: 3).

It has similarly and to my mind as implausibly been argued
in the past that Homeric Greeks—or even Greeks in general—
lacked any clear sense of their own single identities.

> We believe that a man advances from an earlier situation by an act
> of his own will, through his own power. . . . [Homer] has no
> recourse but to say that the responsibility lies with a god. . . .
> Homeric man was not yet awakened to the fact [*sic*] that he
> possesses in his own soul the source of his powers. . . . He receives
> them as a natural and fitting donation from the gods. (Snell 1953:
> 21)

The evidence for this assertion, and for the even wilder claim
made by Jaynes (1976: 84) that 'at one time human nature
was split in two, an executive part called a god, a follower part
called a man', is not very strong, though the idea clearly has
its attractions for the over-imaginative psycho-historian.
What interests me here is that Snell, and his followers, seem to
assume that the belief they attribute to the Greeks is obviously

false, that there is instead a single being straightforwardly identifiable with a particular material object with incontestable temporal and spatial boundaries such that it is self-evident that all the powers, moods, faculties, and thoughts associated with that object actually 'belong' in some clear sense to that single being. This is supposed to be self-evidently true even though there is no sign that the being thus postulated can actually control its moods, powers, thoughts, and faculties. As Dodds remarked, before going on to dismiss such failure to admit to one's 'real' ownership of thoughts, 'Often a man is conscious of no observation or reasoning which has led up to the recognition, the insight, the memory, the brilliant or perverse idea—but how then can he call them his?' (Dodds 1951: 11) How indeed, especially when we have no coherent theory to explain just how material events can issue in just these mental happenings? It is also obvious that the identity and limits of any complex organism or aggregate—which is what the human creature is now supposed to be—must be a matter of 'more or less', not 'all or nothing'. Even at a material level, biologists can point out that things which we habitually regard as unitary systems are better conceived as aggregations of smaller units: what looks like (and, in a sense, certainly is) a swarm of fish or flock of birds may not really be managed by any unitary purpose shared among the individuals. Its apparent unanimity is a by-product of the self-serving choices of many individual organisms, as they jostle to get away from predators, or to take advantages of the updraft from the leader's wings. Such reductionism is so popular a stance that it is very puzzling that it should be considered obvious that there are real human individuals who are not thus decomposable, or even that 'we' ordinarily or inevitably suppose there are. If Homeric man did address his *thumos*, or experience waves of anger or lust or sudden insight as things 'from outside', it certainly does not follow that he was in any comic or psychotic 'dissociated state': he simply spoke rather differently about the common human condition. As Nilsson acknowledged, 'pluralistic teaching about the soul is founded in the nature of things and only our habits of thought make it surprising that man should have several "souls" ' (1949: 89 cited by Dodds 1951: 174 n. 111).

Multiple personality is humanity in its natural condition. In other cultures these multiple personalities have names, locations, energies, functions, voices, angel and animal forms, even theoretical formulations as different kinds of soul. (Hillman 1983: 51)

Just as someone in the midst of a crowd, holding a mirror and looking at it sees not only his own face but also the faces of those looking in the mirror with him, so someone who looks into his own heart sees in it not only his own state, but also the black faces of the demons. (Heyschios, in *Philokalia* 1979: 166)

Atomistic reductionism offers one challenge to the supposed or supposedly popular unity of the self, Platonic realism another. When Apuleius defines a good *daimon* as 'animus virtute perfectus' (*De Deo Socratis* 15. 150 ff.: Nitzsche 1975: 31) he is speaking at once of a discarnate intellect and of what moderns would see only as an abstract universal, not a concrete one. But we can, and do, recognize the *same* moods, thoughts, powers, and faculties in association with different material objects. It may be that when we try to explain what is going on we must abandon our implicit belief in effective universals and rely instead upon the particular local mechanism that gave the misleading impression that one and the same Form was present on many particular occasions: nominalism may be the truth (though I doubt it). But if we take that step, and rule out any appeal to gods, spirits, fairies, forms, we must also rule out appeals to a unitary self (ourself) that manifests upon separate particular occasions. If an accurate ontology contains no forms of the kind that 'Homeric man' imagined, but only 'punctiform particulars' that happen to remind us (who?) of each other, neither does it contain individual human selves with obvious boundaries (see Clark 1986a). Nor does it contain any of the words which nominalists imagine might replace an older, realistic belief in forms: how, after all, does it help to replace the 'same form' which manifests as one in many by the 'same word' that also must manifest as one in many?

That the 7-year-old whom my mother remembers by my name was *me* is not, in modern terms, a fact of nature which I would be merely ignorant or deluded in denying: it is as much a socio-legal convention as the claim that this suit is mine. Identity, on modern terms, is as much a supervenient and contestable property as moral righteousness. If this is so, then it is simply silly to complain or sneer if other peoples have had different rules, especially if our actual rules are a lot more like the ones attributed to them than those which patronizing commentators claim for us. What dogmatists insist is a single, simple entity (though they decline to believe any of the metaphysical doctrines which are implied by such a dogma) can as well be described as a battleground, a complex apparatus, a chimera.

All of which suggests not that the Japanese or the Homeric Greeks either were or thought themselves to be quite different sorts of things from what 'we' are or think ourselves to be, but simply that they sometimes emphasized, or took seriously, a slightly different range of human experience from that which our systematizers have preferred. What Kipling's poem reveals is not, in the end, the radical incommensurability of different languages and cultures, but their similarity. Crudely, table manners differ—but all human kinds have table manners; marital arrangements differ—but all human kinds have marriages, and also have adulteries; even the topography of the soul may differ, but we can all recognize ourselves even in what seem to us, whoever we are, distorted mirrors.

Plato's insight—to which I shall be returning many times—was that there were real samenesses present many times over in the world of mundane experience, that these samenesses were the truly real things, that 'I'—so far as it names anything—names a thing like that, a living form inextricably bound up in larger unities, called gods and *daimons*. If anti-realists are (absurdly) right, there is no harm following Plato's example; if they are wrong then something very much like Platonism is correct. But that is a larger issue still.

Aliens and Homely Animals

Hume was clearly wrong to think that all genuinely 'reason-able' people thought and felt as he or other Hanoverian gentlemen thought they did themselves, that differences in expressed priorities and properties were merely by-products of changed circumstances, or of superstition, not of any different 'human nature'. It is quite right to emphasize by way of contrast and corrective that we need to make a difficult imaginative leap in entering the worlds and souls of other ages and societies. What would, perhaps, be neurotic self-abnegation in Hume's society would be high virtue in less gentlemanly days: Bellarmine's half-serious quip that he would endure the bite of vermin since he had eternity to look forward to, whereas their felicity could only be in this life, excites Hume's ridicule. A modern man who, on hearing a gospel reading about the rich young ruler, walks across England to become a monk, is promptly certified (see Drury 1973: 124 f.): but even if (as seems to me improbable) he was insane, it does not follow that someone who, in one sense, did much the same thing in the thirteenth century was lunatic (though St Francis's family doubtless thought he was).

A humble deference to other days and climes and characters is virtuous, but we should not so exaggerate the problems as to let it be thought that those ages are in any literal sense quite alien to us, and not to be judged by standards that we can find within our own 'inherited conglomerate'. However hard we try we have not yet discovered any speaking peoples whose experience cannot be mapped on ours. D'Arcy Thompson's demonstration (1917) that different animal forms can be shown as the same forms variously mapped, by altering the geometry of the several co-ordinates, provides a useful metaphor.

Indeed, that much is almost obvious. A gaggle of somethings whom we could not understand by suitable distortions of our own experience would not even be recognizable as familiar animals—for of course our empathy extends to other mammals, vertebrates, and even further across the biological spectrum. Much of what is common stock in human kinds is part of our mammalian or vertebrate heritage, or part of what is necessary to any animal kind. Any animal must place some limits on what is itself, or its own—though we should do well to notice that those limits may not always remain, or ever be, the same as those we think we have. It is not obvious that any neurologically isolated animal (one whose motions are physically determined by the interaction of its environment with its central control mechanisms) will have 'its own' survival as a central or preferential policy on all possible occasions. Indeed, we can be quite sure that it will not. When the motivating mechanisms that evolution has bred into all such creatures are themselves made into objects of cognition—when the self-reflexive mind makes its appearance—we can say that such animals will not always identify themselves with their obvious physical boundaries, with what is packed within their sack of skin. Such creatures will not be, nor think of themselves as being, ends in themselves or independent atomies. 'For the Bantu man never appears as an isolated individual, as an independent entity: every man, every individual forms a link in a chain of vital forces' (Placide Temprel, cited by Lienhardt 1985: 144). 'Bantu Philosophy' is just like ours, unless we are deracinated modernists. Social and self-aware animals will experience themselves, as humans always have, as finite and dependent functionaries, playgrounds of the shifting moods and releasers and inhibitors we label 'gods'. The notion that each one of them contains a unitary self, distinct from all other selves and owing itself an absolute devotion, is—to say the least—a late comer.

> All is dependent [upon another], naught is independent,
> This is the pure truth, we speak it out plainly.
> If I mention One, Self-sufficient, Independent,
> You will know to Whom I refer.
> All is bound up with all, there is no escaping
> This bond, so consider carefully what I say.
>
> (Ibn Arabi 1980: 57; written 1223–40)

So it is not only those 'we' classify as human who are overwhelmingly likely to be non-alien. No familiar animal is beyond our empathy: an aphorism that hovers between the biologistic and the a priori. If there were things that were wholly alien we could not even begin to think of what they were; if they are the products of the same sort of evolution as ourselves they could not be wholly alien, however gross the distorting mirror we should have to imagine in order to enter their world. Even the efforts of fabulists and psycho-historians, expectably enough, have not turned up real aliens—but they will doubtless go on trying, just because we plainly want to find an Archimedean point beyond the world even though we know full well that if there really were such aliens they could not understand nor comment on us at all. Psycho-historian and fabulist are groping around the imagined limits of the world, and do us a service, even if it is not the one they wish. What they do is show us that our limits are not as narrow as we once had thought, that we could be out there in that almost alien world.

The alien or almost alien worlds composed by science fiction writers are very often hierarchical or caste societies, or ones (equivalently?) whose members look much further forward or back than the birthdays of each atomy. Often enough they see the world as ruled by varying principles of light or dark, encapsulate their world-views in stories rather than in systematic treatises, and endure radical discontinuities of purpose and essential nature. In so far as such fables often themselves encapsulate contemporary Westron fears, it is noticeable that feudal or communistic, 'self-less' or militaristic societies are being described as imaginative rivals of 'our own', which is represented by indirection. Those fables in turn affect how we see Soviet or Japanese competitors in this 'real' world. What we are groping for is a convincing picture of the Shadow, the Self that we are not, in order that we may find out what we are, or hope to be. The same function, as Said 1978 has pointed out, was (and is) performed by Western images of the 'Orient'. 'Modern individualistic liberalism' and its associated psychodrama needs those loathly opposites against which to try its strength—or perhaps the more traditional psychology and polity that I aim to describe has invented modern individualistic liberalism as its own fantastic opposite.

2

Introspection and Experiment

The Inner and the Outer

The society of strangers, or disconnected and deracinated aliens, which has served the purposes of political philosophers disinclined to take their start from 'the inherited conglomerate' has its more openly individualistic analogue in the image of the solitary sage, hunting for the truth that his society has hidden or forgotten or not known. It is a familiar response that science or scholarship in general is not quite so much the product of such solitary or misanthropic intelligences as our myths suggest: science is a communal endeavour, and not to be created all over again by any individual, however brilliant. Even if there are individual innovators, scorned by their contemporaries, they only embody in some sidelong mode the knowledge and practice of an earlier age or larger community. No individual shorn of her community has any separate access to the divine intellect, no merely private way to truth.

It follows, so it has been supposed, that sound methodology requires the acceptance of public and repeatable experiment, that truth lies in the common, not in private dream. As Heracleitos said in one of his less enigmatic aphorisms: 'For those who've woken up there is one common world; each sleeper's turned aside to a private one' (22 B 89 DK).

And from that in turn it follows or seems to follow that introspection cannot show us even how our own souls are made or manifested. 'Looking within' was the preferred technique of Hobbes or Hume, but later and more sophisticated empiricists do not rely on personal self-consciousness, or even admit that any such thing exists. Personal conscience and the inner light have been so exalted in the political sphere as to suggest that all those who are moved by humble loyalty to crown or creed must be dangerous and unthinking zombies. But in the realm of science and scholarship it is the whole community that determines what is to be believed: what only appears to one observer cannot be accepted as evidence, even if the appearance carries, for that one, the compelling quality of immediate conviction. It follows that if there were truths over and above what could be commonly or publicly recognized, we should be debarred from acknowledging them (which is, as James observed (1897: 28), a thoroughly irrational rule). If the sage could speak we could not understand him.

Despite the efforts of eliminative materialists and Wittgensteinians most of us remain convinced that each of us does have some privileged access to a realm behind her eyes, that introspection does reveal a realm closed off from public commentary. Anti-realists and materialists are actually both engaged in eliminating the fear of uncertainty by denying any gap between what we think and what is really true: anti-realists deny the latter any extra-mental being; eliminative materialists deny the former any non-material being. Both—in effect—surrender to Pyrrhonian scepticism. The very attempt to make everything a matter of public judgement amounts to an attempt to evade the truism that in the last resort every human being is on her own. Lienhardt, whose description of 'Bantu philosophy', as I have already observed, is—as he says—entirely familiar to traditional, socially conscious Europeans, also cites a Congolese proverb that 'none may put his arm into his neighbour's inside' (1985: 146)! Indeed that reality, once we begin to think of it, turns out not to hide behind our eyes, as if my perceptual universe, maintained through my senses, were public property and my imagination not. Jung is in error in supposing that it is a mark of 'primitives' to 'confuse' the inner and the outer realms: the real question is, where is the supposed 'outer'? Even if my percepts, duly filled out by imagination and hypothesis, do tell me about a world in which not I alone, but uncounted others live, it remains obvious that those percepts are not numerically the same as yours. 'Naïve realism' of the kind that insists that the world-as-I-perceive-it is identical with what causes me and all of you to perceive it as we do (so that if you report things otherwise you must be wrong) is, as Collingwood remarked, only another name for human stupidity. Berkeleian, or scholastic, realism, as I shall expound it in another volume, has the merit that the naïve realist would seek of denying that our percepts are unreal, but also acknowledges that our several perceptual universes are distinct. How things are for the sheep-tick, the content of its perceptual universe, is not to be equated with the universe that environs tick and sheep and shepherd.

> It was a hard thing to undo this knot.
> The rainbow shines, but only in the thought
> of him that looks. Yet not in that alone,
> for who makes rainbows by invention?
> And many standing round a waterfall
> see one bow each, yet not the same to all,
> but each a hand's breadth further than the next
> which yet is in the eye or in the thought.
> It was a hard thing to undo this knot.
>
> (Hopkins 1970: 129 f.)

The common world is not as easily accessible as naïve empiricists have thought. Berkeley's view (*Siris* 264: 1948: v. 124) was well summarized, as Walker (1985: 123) has pointed out, by Kant: 'all knowledge through the senses and through experience is nothing but illusion, and only in the ideas of pure understanding and reason is truth' (Kant 1953: 145)—though Berkeley would have called such 'ideas' notions and emphasized that the error of sensualists lies not in the percepts—which are in themselves as real creatures as anything else—but in the mistaken judgement of the perceiver, of supposing that her percepts are self-sustaining. Access to the common is not direct: we may naïvely believe that 'we' are solid, coloured, noisy objects rattling around within a directly perceived universe, and so ignore the vast worlds of delight hidden away in others. Birds are not small brown fluttering objects, any more than persons are identical with what we see or touch or hear.

> How do you know but ev'ry Bird that cuts the airy way,
> is an immense world of delight, clos'd by your senses five?
>
> (Blake 1966: 150)

As Berkeley said, no one ever strictly sees a person, for persons are not someone else's visual ideas (*Alciphron:* 1948: iii. 149). 'To know that other beings have an equal right with us to say "I"—to know it completely, such a thing is supernatural. As supernatural perhaps as the belief in the Eucharist. And as in the case of the Eucharist, the organ for such belief is supernatural love' (Weil 1956: i. 295). Which raises a general question about the possible modes of discovery.

It is by now so much the fashion to denounce anything that can be called or miscalled 'dualism', that even commentators who would deny that they are materialists, or even, sometimes, atheists, regularly suggest that dualism appeals only to the senile or the doctrinaire. Perhaps there are some dualisms that deserve the jibe. To me, however, a dogmatic monism, an insistence that there is 'only one sort of real thing', that all forms of discourse and all items of knowledge must be captured in a single formula, sounds as metaphysically wild as any ancient creed, and sits very ill with the similarly fashionable thought that we should prefer pragmatic and undogmatic methods to an absolute insistence on there being one single truth. If there is no one right way, or none that we possess, it is, as James remarked of another fashionable dictate, 'a piece of idle fantasticality' (James 1897: 30) to preach that every kind of dualism, however useful or immediately evident, must be disavowed. As it happens, a dualism of discourse is very widely advocated (so that physical description and personalistic description of the doings of our species are simultaneously affirmed, without any serious attempt to provide a unified theory of what goes on and/or what is done). That topic will engross me in a later chapter, when I observe that we thereby impute to human beings, at least, two natures in one person.

But 'dualism', in any case, covers a multitude. There is a distinction between my perceptual universe, which un-doubtedly includes far more than twinges, murmurs, aches, and flashing lights, and yours. My universe is richer than imaginable others because my imagination gives body, history, and significance to the 'bare' data that just any abstract percipient might possess. We do not actually perceive flat coloured shapes from which we distantly infer a solid

universe, any more—as Berkeley pointed out—than one who
knows how to read first sees a mysterious set of shapes and
then laboriously decodes a meaning. We grasp things as
having unseen back parts, histories, and evaluative structures.
An aboriginal story-teller, walking through the land, plucks
his tribe's stories from the landmarks that he passes. All this is
regularly reported as if it somehow rebutted the claim that my
percepts are not you, but should actually tend to confirm it: I
might be prepared to suggest that the heroes of the Dreamtime
hide in cliff or tree to prompt the story-teller, but I like
maverick hypotheses. It is just not true, *pace* Evans-Pritchard,
that 'no Greek, except on the stage, ever saw cloud-gathering
Zeus' (1962: 53; see Duerr 1985: 347), even if 'really' there
was no Zeus there to be 'seen'. But even I would have to admit
that there are plenty of wild stories told about our nearest
neighbours. If what I immediately, and prejudicially, observe
is—let us suppose—an amorous young woman who is only
pretending to refuse, it is clear that my perceptual universe,
and the image of that woman, is erotically suffused: but is it so
obvious, to the sane intelligence, that so must the young
woman be? Someone in a temper may perceive all manner of
grudges and hostile actions: but part of any honourable code
of conduct is an attempt to judge things fairly, to remember
that things as they are lie on the far side of a veil.

What lies on that far side of course is not wholly lacking in
significance: the dualism which moderns think most obvious
lies between the universe as it is humanly perceived and the
'bare facts'. Those who would know the truth, we are advised,
must conceive a world drained of all affect, all 'merely
subjective' colouring. In Steig's story of Howard the Duck, a
frog 'shows him around Manhattan'—but duck and frog are
travelling through the sewers, and never see anything 'up top'.
As humans and as mammals we perceive a world rich with
attractions and with dangers, teleological structures, and
details to be filled out by empathetic imagination. In personal
and political affairs, it is usually acknowledged, we cannot get
by without these fair illusions. But in the world of truth, so we
are told, all knowledge comes by describing what goes on
without affect, without involvement, without any human
sense of value or importance. To see things 'objectively' is to

see them without reverence—and thence, question-beggingly, infer the real absence of anything meriting our reverence (as Monod does: 1972). Time and causality themselves, on some accounts, are not part of the fabric of the world; ethics and identity at least are not. The truth is approached by cutting out all that is merely personal: our sense of what it might be like to be our neighbour, or our pet, our tree, our elementary particle may serve a brief heuristic function, but tells us nothing 'scientific' about what things are. That anyone should ever suppose that such truth is humanly worth knowing I can only regard as a superstitious relic of past metaphysics. There can at least, if there are no objective wrongs, be no objective wrong in turning our eyes away from it.

Things as they are and things as I perceive them are not numerically or formally the same. One much-touted route to Things as They Are is, nowadays, the way of alienation, equated without much argument with experimental method. Experiments, it is supposed, will work for anyone, of whatever irrelevant moral character or imaginative insight. What they reveal (for anything less would betoken an ill-designed experiment) is that normal human values have no effect upon the way things are, and that there is no need for animistic metaphysics in the explanation of the motion of the planets, growth of trees, or movement of even 'higher' animals (which are in fact no higher than bacteria). Experiments are designed, as Duerr points out, to exclude demons (1985: 335). Some few philosophers have tried to bend their minds around the final gloss: that scientists are not truly described as seeking out the truth by hypothetico-deductive reasoning and objective experiment. All that *truly* happens is the 'motion' of whatever particles or waves or superstrings, which somehow makes an illusion of mental being to deceive the faithful. I did not write nor speak, and neither did you read, a sentence then—any more than the eldil Malacandra is responsible for the orbit of the planet Mars, or thunder betokens Olympian anger. If such philosophers are what they say they are, it would not make sense even to compliment them on their sincerity. Weil's comment on this kind of 'naturalized epistemology':

Theories spring up as it were at random, and there is survival of the fittest (i.e. of those that catch the fancy of the village of savants).

Such a science as this can well be a form of *élan vital*, but certainly not a form of the search for truth. (Weil 1987: 247)

So grant for a moment that there is a gap, which all of us have regularly transcended on particular occasions but which yawns before us still, between things as they are and things as we now perceive them. And grant, for the sake of carrying on with any sensible conversation, that we cannot eliminate all meaning from the way things are, or practise the way of alienation without obvious and rank dishonesty. How do we, from time to time, transcend our limits?

Experimental Methods

The hypothetico-deductive method, of course, has no necessary connection with the objectivist mythology to which I have just been referring, nor has it any special connection with those disciplines that are self-identified as 'scientific'. The weird assumption that only those with a 'scientific' training can actually think is as obvious a piece of self-serving ideology as that of any ancient priesthood. What is common to every intellectual inquiry is the wish to find a reasonable explanation for whatever range of data currently require explanation. To be reasonable is to be more or less compatible with already accepted theory, to provide a more elegant model from which further predictions can be elicited, to explain, along with the immediate data, why other theories have done as well as they have, and to offer the possibility of additional refinement, exploration, hints toward analogous explanations in other areas, and so on. What is a reasonable sort of explanation for the motions of elementary particles would not be a reasonable sort for the behaviour of human beings: misplaced animism may be an intellectual sin, but so is misplaced mathematization. A well-established theory and methodology in any area allows relatively large amounts of work to be done by rote, even by formula, but it is always open to the creative intelligence to take a good theory that unpredictable move further on, to apply it where nothing in the original theory had said that it should be applied, and still make it work. 'Reason, or the ratio of all that we have already known, is not the same that it shall be when we know more' (Blake 1966: 97). But there is—or so we must believe—a reasoning capacity that gets us further on than what could rationally be deduced from previous theory. 'As none by travelling over known lands can find out the unknown, so from already acquired knowledge Man could not acquire more: therefore an universal Poetic Genius exists' (Blake 1966: 98). That last, abrupt deduction must wait for its explication.

The process by which we chiefly find out what is, or what could sensibly be thought to be, is a combination of more or less inspired guesswork, combined with rigorous testing of the workings of our guess—though we must always recognize that such tests are never simple, that we never in fact, however controlled our laboratory, manage to test just one hypothesis. We have enough historical experience of peoples who have got off on the wrong foot, and never thought to abandon their oldest, most honourable guesses, to give emotional weight to the pessimistic inference that all our present theories are likely to be thought both false and faintly silly in a thousand years. 'And the rigorous belief that in its own essential and innermost nature this is a strictly impersonal world may prove to be the very defect that our descendants will be most surprised at in our boasted science' (James 1897: 327). Even those elements of present theory that have been retained in almost the same shape for many generations of investigators cannot now mean quite what they once did, in a different context, to a different age. All this applies to historical or philosophical investigation quite as much as to astronomy or physics.

So what is miscalled 'scientific method', namely the formulation and testing of hypotheses to explain and help predict some field of data, is not tied to any dogmatically impersonalist method. To rule out intentional explanation, or empathetic identification, as routes to knowledge amounts to a process of self-blinding for which there is historical explanation but very little philosophical justification. No serious Western astronomer, no doubt, while in professional mode, would explain dark patches in the heavens by reference to interstellar civilizations engaged in trapping all their luminary's output, rather than to unintended or accidental clouds of interstellar dust. There are several good reasons for this policy, but none of them even begins to show that we would be factually mistaken if we began to act upon the more baroque hypothesis—as Soviet scientists are apparently inclined to do. Ockham's Razor (that entities are not to be multiplied beyond necessity) or Morgan's Canon (that animal behaviour is to be explained in terms of the least complex, most 'primitive' motivations that are adequate to the task) are good ideas, but their application here rests upon an unargued assumption that intelligence is less 'likely' than dust.

I said 'unargued': one usual response is to say that what is complex must arise only from what is simple, and has therefore automatically less chance of existence than the mere simples from which it might arise, and that 'intelligence' is obviously more 'complex' than the dust, as requiring the existence of many-celled and neurologically sophisticated organisms bound together in a socio-historical web. These theses, despite their resemblance to the historicism of my previous chapter, are not so obvious to me: at the very least it should be noticed that ancient philosophers would have denied them both, and that their present popularity is hardly more than an aftermath of the post-medieval rebellion against scholasticism. Even today scientists seem to feel bound to indulge their occasional contempt for Aristotle, without ever bothering to find out what he said. Perhaps they are wise: it is never comfortable to notice that one's firmest convictions are contestable.

The problem for epistemologists remains: what sort of universe must this really be if we are to have much chance of finding out about it? A rigorously impersonal world, in which they are—by definition—no odds in favour of the emergence of experiencing and intending beings, and no reason to expect such beings as by chance emerge (if this is even possible) to have any key to underlying principles of being that would guide their guesses right, must always be less likely to produce such beings than a world 'personal' from the beginning. It seems to me, therefore, that the hypothesis of an essentially 'personal' beginning always has the edge over the alternative.

It could never be sensible to expect an impersonal universe to produce persons having any epistemic key to anything (at best) beyond what might preserve their genes. Those who believe in such a universe should not rationally expect there to be any such beings, and should not, therefore, suppose themselves to be such beings. Those who believe in an originally impersonal universe should not suppose that their belief is realistically true.

It is no reply at all to say that although we could not have expected this or any other outcome, we must accept that it has happened: we do not, and obviously could not, know from experience that it *has* happened, but only that we can reconstruct a more or less consistent story about what is from the buzzing confusion of our actual experience. Believing that this story is correct as well as coherent would itself be an unwarranted claim if the story told us that we would tell just the same story even if it were actually incorrect. But in a universe where the only selective pressure towards the development of 'intelligence' is, at best, to get the next meal and avoid being one, there is no reason to acquire true beliefs about the world at large. We might as well expect to find that honey-bees always included a map of the United States inside their hives, or that there 'really were' sermons in stones and books in the running brooks. As a good realist and rationalist, I prefer to believe that the universe is of its nature such as to produce the little enclaves and distorting mirrors that we experience as human consciousness, expressly intended to grow up to know.

The great principle of the Infinite Intelligibility of the Universe is the cornerstone of Scientific Theism; and its warrant is universal human experience, purified, consolidated and organized in the scientific method. (Abbot 1885: 125)[1]

But can I now turn that reasonable hypothesis around? The strength or purported strength of impersonalism is that it offered an epistemology: so curb your passions and immediate

---

[1] It is worth remarking that this book was strongly recommended by C. S. Peirce (see Boler 1963, after Peirce 1934: 4.50). The Bodleian copy was—in 1987—uncut.

empathy as to conceive that everything is the unintended effect of merely mathematically describable motions (carefully ignoring all unpleasant questions about the imaginable scope of human mathematics). Such a methodology is a piece of idle fantasticality when applied to our human neighbours or even a captive goldfish, and its proponents do not even succeed in applying it consistently in the regions where it has some use. But the presumed absence of an idealist epistemology has left this travesty in possession of the field. 'Presumed absence' only. One does not transcend the immediate illusion of supposing that one's erotic fancy is identical with a someone out there in the world by making believe that women are impersonal mechanisms! On the contrary, such self-transcendence comes with an awareness of what it is for her, the person represented in one's waking dream, to be. With that realization the image grows in depth and richness until, one can conceive as an unattainable limit, it contains all the world is for that person. Hua-Yen Buddhism offers the metaphor of Indra's Net, each jewel of which reflects all other jewels, and the multiple reflections contained in them. Each of us, as each of us is a world, is a partial refraction of the totality of worlds, and the pursuit of knowledge is an attempt to contain more rather than less, to appreciate the richness of other worlds and not to pare down one's own to an abstract formula. 'My sentient experience samples the character of Reality at large' (Fawcett 1916: 69).

This process of increasing knowledge does indeed require something rather like the asceticism that objectivists propose: we need to disentangle our private dream from the larger dreaming, not to be misled by personal or social projections. That was implicit in the example I have been sketching, the refusal to take one's own first fancy as the truth about another. But if we were left with no empathetic understanding once the erotic charge was dissipated, that would be no help at all. What happens is that a deeper layer of the imagination is achieved, a better understanding from within of the body language and articulate speech of others. Once again, as an unattainable limit, we can conceive of an intelligence that sees out of the eyes of all things, that comprehends all points of view, for which all opaque personalities are open books. It is important, even while conceiving this, that we should not imagine that we have attained such a condition. That, after all, is the very error, of naïve realism, from which we begin, of thinking that how things are for Us is how they are. It is also worth noting that, human beings being what they are, the wish to 'get inside' another's subjectivity is all too easily transformed into erotic curiosity.

This outline of how we come to know each other does not amount simply to understanding others 'by analogy' with our known selves: on the contrary, the shock of understanding others enlarges our knowledge of what we are. That is why the technique applied to non-human subjects is not anthropomorphic: *anthropos* is one form only (or better still a multitude of forms) of conscious being, and those who enlarge their consciousness to take in how things are for dogs or cats or bats come to know the mammal beneath the skin. Is there some limit to the technique beyond which merely 'objective' reasonings are valid? Can we find out about 'the' world of physical science and mathematically describable principle by such enlargements of personal consciousness? The thought has been common enough in poetry, and Hopkins invented a word for it, namely 'selving' (see Moore 1944: 189). And consider Kathleen Raine's injunction—

> Sleep at the tree's root, where the night is spun
> into the stuff of worlds, listen to the winds,
> the tides, and the night's harmonies, and know
> all that you knew before you began to forget,
> before you became estranged from your own being.
>
> (Raine 1956: 174)

We may even remember 'mystics' who have said much the same, like Aurobindo:

One begins to feel others too as a part of oneself or varied repetitions of oneself, the same self modified by Nature in other bodies. Or at the least as living in the larger universal self which is henceforth one's own greater reality. All things in fact begin to change their nature and appearance; one's whole experience of the world is radically different from that of those who are shut up in their personal selves. (Cited by Satprem 1968: 172 f.)

What has been forgotten is that the thought lay at the very beginning of 'modern science': 'Fundamental laws of motion and of rest are laws of a mathematical nature. We find and discover them not in Nature, but in ourselves, in our mind, in our memory, as Plato long ago has taught us' (Galileo: cited by Koyre 1968: 13, 42)—not that Galileo's rhetorical contrast between Nature and Mind bears close examination.

Modernist rhetoric, to the effect that old, 'mystical' epistemologies have failed to compete with objectivist, experimental epistemologies, is based upon a profound misconception. It may sound as if the mystic claims an infallibility which the working scientist or scholar disowns, but Aurobindo expressly rejects the idea that we could ever be immune to error. And Fawcett, a neglected Western philosopher who advanced a similar scheme, remarked that 'private imagining may collide with that cosmic imagining bodied forth in the structure of Nature, as when a geologist, enamoured of a dream, affirms some belief regardless of the testimony of the rocks' (Fawcett 1921: 7; he was perhaps being marginally unfair to Philip Gosse). Innovative science, conversely, depends on 'the imaginative vision and faith in the ultimate success' (Planck: cited by Beveridge 1953: 55). 'Genius is revealed in a delicate feeling which correctly foresees the laws of natural phenomena' (Bernard 1949: 43).[2] 'The way of intuition, helped by a feeling for the order lying behind appearance' is indispensable, as Einstein said (Beveridge 1953: 57), for any realistic concept of the universe. Without it we must remain, like Plato's prisoners, making our untutored guesses about the shadow play. With it, as we seek to imagine what it would be like to ride on the crest of a light wave, or what it is to be a protein molecule, we enlarge our fragmentary minds towards what It was in the beginning. 'Our evolutionary journey is a slow reconquest of what we had exiled, a revival of Memory' (Satprem 1968: 174).

So to understand things we should start from the understanding. To perfect our understanding we should seek to found ourselves more securely on what lies 'within'. Instead of

[2] An author no less worth listening to on this point simply because he was an unrepentant and entirely callous vivisector.

putting our faith in 'outward things', and supposing that we must depend on something that is to be found within the house, as an object among others, we must seek the true Self, the one thing that no house can contain—its own foundations. We must understand how much of the house as we find it is a product of our merely idiosyncratic perceptions (rats and creepy-crawly things, for example, are not evil 'in themselves', but only as we perceive them). Things are not good or bad as they do or do not appeal to our own little tastes. We must 're-educate our imaginings', by going 'deeper' and by feeling our way, imaginatively, into the great structures of traditional religion, the larger house. This attempt is, precisely, an emotional one: it is an attempt to awaken in us, or to allow the expression in us, of larger and more convivial emotions than the narrow and self-reinforcing horrors that most of us are plagued by.

Which is where Blake comes in: God is the Poetic Faculty, the Imagination Itself, and not to be finally identified with any of Its products.

We of Israel [said Blake's Ezekiel] taught that the Poetic Genius (as you now call it) was the first principle and all the others merely derivative, which was the cause of our despising the Priests and Philosophers of other countries, and prophecying that all Gods would at last be proved to originate in ours and to be the tributaries of the Poetic Genius. (Blake 1966: 153)

It is easy for modernists to assume that when Blake said again that 'all deities reside in the human breast' he was thinking of humans as they are naturally thought to be, and that theology was a 'mere' poetic fiction. But it is 'the true Man, he being the Poetic Genius' that is the source. 'All sects of Philosophy are from the Poetic Genius adapted to the weakness of every individual', and that Genius, that Man, is an individual reality, not an abstract universal. Blake, in fact, was writing in the ancient tradition of metaphysical theism. The impersonal universe constructed, for whatever reason, by objectivizing scientists—and one reason among many has undoubtedly been the wish to leave 'nature' and natural creatures free to serve our purposes—is a thing that we have made, as much an idol as any wooden toy denounced by Isaiah. To suppose that something we have thus made up is the ground and explanation of all our experience is as absurd. More so: 'The fetishists are superior to us: they are infinitely less idolatrous than we. They have a religious respect for a piece of carved wood which is beautiful, and to which beauty imparts an eternal significance' (Weil 1987: 247). 'The imagination opens, now as always, into heavens and hells of the mind, beyond which lies boundless mystery' (Raine 1982: 23).

Introspection, in brief, is the beginning of the process of discovery: the mathematical and ideal models we uncover in ourselves, and which give added richness to the world of common day, are either more or less useful projections or else approximations to the real causes of all experience. If they are the latter, as I myself am happy to suppose, we have good reason to accept that they exist as imaginative symbols in the cosmic imagining, and good reason to take seriously the possibility that a dedicated and trained endeavour might discover more of those 'giants who formed the sensual world into its existence now live in it in chains' (Blake 1966: 155).

I have already hinted that the imagination we interrogate is otherwise known as Memory, a memory that reaches further down than our conscious being. Augustine's apparently mysterious comment that that is where God is to be found takes shape within that prior awareness of the mind's mountains. I shall be returning to that topic in my fifth chapter. Here I wish to recall the images fed into modern mythology by the philosopher and fabulist Olaf Stapledon, especially one of his later fictions, *The Flames*.

The Flames

The Flames is a brief and well-crafted fable which encapsulates many of Stapledon's concerns and characteristic ironies. Patrick McCarthy correctly observes that 'as an example of controlled and sustained irony *The Flames* is without parallel among Stapledon's works' (1982: 155). Thos, the critical minnow-watcher, presents and comments on the narrative of Cass, the speculative generalist. Cass, after years of seeking to

see and understand things 'from the inside', by telepathic or
mystical means, seems to himself to have been addressed by a
living flame, hidden in a pebble plucked from a cold, snow-
shrouded landscape. It turns out that there are such creatures,
salamanders, born in the sun's troposphere and condemned to
live out a cold and intermittent existence on solid earth since
the planets were formed. The late world war, and its manifold
fires, have brought them out of hibernation in the dust of the
air, and they sense the possibility of forming a symbiotic
alliance with us: we to provide the environment within which
they can live, they to provide the mental stability and
community awareness we lack. This sort of symbiotic pattern
is many times repeated in Stapledon's work. If we cannot
agree, the flames' other option is to instigate nuclear spasm:
'then at last, with the whole planet turned into a single atomic
bomb, and all the incandescent continents hurtling into space,
we should have for a short while conditions almost as good as
those of our golden age in the sun' (1947: 61). Cass is on the
point of agreeing to act as the flames' ambassador, when he
learns that his own marriage had been deliberately destroyed
by the flames (and his wife incidentally driven to suicide) so
that he might be a suitably single-minded instrument of their
purposes (the Neptunian hero of *Last Men in London* had done
the same, less violently, to his victim, unrebuked). Cass
concludes that this proves the flames' real ill-will, destroys the
flame with a glass of cold water (the flames turn to revivable
dust if slowly extinguished, but perish forever if suddenly
doused), and sets himself to warn humankind of the deadly
peril they stand in. He is eventually incarcerated in an
asylum, where the flames again convince him that their
intentions were good. Meanwhile, however, their more lucid
companions, in the sun, have (as usual in Stapledon)
discovered that Reality 'was wholly alien to the spirit, and
wholly indifferent to the most sacred values of the awakened
minds of the cosmos' (1947: 79), and are undergoing a
desperate religious war in which the flames' original pious
agnosticism is lost. Cass, now converted to that typically
Stapledonian position, is threatened by flames converted in
their turn to a militant theism. Cass dies in a fire, victim of
homicide or, as Thos supposes, his own deranged endeavour.

The swirling confusion of Stapledonian history is here compressed into one man's life, and the struggle to live lucidly, without self-deception, is allowed its full ironical perversity. Who is deceived? Who is sane? Allegorically, of course, the flames are simply those technological powers whose use may lead to utopia or to disaster. Or else they are a shifting image of the individual-in-community, less inclined than we to imagine that they are atomic individuals, rather than elements within the global, or the stellar community, and by the same token all too ready to ignore the needs and passions of each such element, and fall into the little death of the hive-mind. Or else again, they are images of the division that concerned Stapledon so often, between sleep and awakened life. The story even allows him what he does not attempt elsewhere, the thought that present individuals are fallen creatures, forever reaching towards a perfection they have lost: 'each new experience came to us with a haunting sense of familiarity and a suspicion that the new version was but a crude and partial substitute for the old' (1947: 37). The flames entertain the project of initiating nuclear spasm, 'through loyalty to the spirit in us', if they should decide that the human species was doomed to self-destruction sooner or later (1947: 60), rather as the Fifth Men of Stapledon's other future history destroy the inhabitants of Venus, on the plea that they are less developed and failing creatures (1963: 252): this slaughter, incidentally, produces in its agents on the one hand an 'unreasoning disgust with humanity' and on the other a 'grave elation' expressing itself in the thought that 'the murder of Venerian life was terrible but right'. Odd John assures his biographer bluntly, 'If we could wipe out your whole species, we would' (1935: 216). The ultimate unreality of time's passage, Stapledon's other constant theme, is not represented in *The Flames*, though the mere fact that millenia of high endeavour are compressed and mirrored in the last few months of one man's life is a little reminder that time does not advance, and the collapse even of the high solar civilization of the flames (contacted at long last by the terrestrial exiles) a warning that there is no security within time.

The unresolved ambiguities of this story—are the flames trustworthy or not, is Cass insane or not, is the god of humane devotion certain to be victorious or not, are the demands of the heart to be accepted alongside the judgements of the mind or not—are what makes it art rather than academic philosophy. But I do not think—as must by now be obvious—that philosophers should always be explicit and precise. What we are seeking to convey is not a doctrine so much as a method, not a single method so much as an awakened eye. A story of wonders that ends 'and it was all a dream' is a cheat; but so is one that ends as a report of matters of fact in the cold light of day. I dislike psychologizing novelists, who would have made of Cass's story merely some sub-Freudian and patronizing tragedy. I prefer the habits of science-fiction writers, who often enough use the trick of imagining that some insane delusion might after all be exactly true. But Stapledon's solution has something to be said for it: 'not such as I had dreamed must the real be, but infinitely more subtle, more dread, more excellent. And infinitely nearer home. Yet, however false the vision in detail of structure, even perhaps in its whole form, in temper surely it was relevant; in temper perhaps it was even true' (1937: 218). In this he echoed Plato's judgement, that it is through the telling of stories, true in temper if not in detail, that we make our philosophical conclusions real to ourselves.

The flames' philosophizing too 'was more imaginative and less conceptual than [ours], more of the nature of art, of myth-construction, which [they] knew to be merely symbolical, not literally true' (1947: 34). They recognize a lack in themselves, or precise analysis and practical intelligence, which they hope will be compensated within a future symbiosis. This too is a common theme in Stapledon: the arachnoids and ichthyoids who are the core of the eventual galactic and cosmic spirit embody the active and contemplative virtues, and are lost without each other. The plant-men who inhabit certain small, hot worlds, similarly, have daytime and night-time phases: 'during the busy night-time they went about their affairs as insulated individuals', and during the day they are united in contemplative ardour with the cosmos. 'In the day-time mode [a plant-man] passed no moral judgement on himself or others. He mentally reviewed every kind of human conduct with detached contemplative joy, as a factor in the universe.

But when night came again, bringing the active nocturnal mood, the calm, day-time insight into himself and others was lit with a fire of moral praise and censure' (1937: 109 f.). The plant-men fail, because after a prolonged attempt to live without contemplation, detached (literally!) from their roots, they swing to the opposite extreme. 'Little by little they gave less and less energy and time to animal pursuits, until at last their nights as well as their days were spent wholly as trees, and the active, exploring, manipulating, animal intelligence died in them forever' (1937: 111)—I presume, without any other evidence than the mere similarity, that this is one of the sources of Tolkien's Ents. The tension is not one that Stapledon ever rationally resolved: on the one hand, the active intelligence wills to produce as fine a future as possible; on the other, the contemplative intelligence, on Stapledon's account, recognizes that this already is the finest universe possible, however ill it suits our animal passions. 'The Man who became a Tree', one of his short stories, ends with the tree's acceptance even of the woodman's axe. In *Odd John*, similarly, John's murderous activity is contrasted with the contemplative Islam of an old boatman, as 'superior' as John but wholly disinclined to try and make any difference to the world. 'Allah wills of his creatures two kinds of service. One is that they should toil to fulfil his active purpose in the world. The other is that they should observe with understanding and praise with discriminating delight the excellent form of his handiwork' (1935: 194). I regret that Stapledon's understanding of this traditional contrast led him to picture even the Starmaker in the guise of a predatory superman.

He recognized in himself an opposition between the little, frightened animal and the realistic intelligence, between everyday concerns and a memory of our cosmic place. It is understandable that some people should resent that intelligence: 'if we were all on board ship and there was trouble among the stewards I can just conceive their chief spokesmen looking with disfavour on anyone who stole away from the fierce debates in the saloon or pantry to take a breather on deck. For up there, he would taste the salt, he would see the vastness of the weather, he would remember that the ship had a whither and a whence. He would remember things like fogs, storms, and what had seemed in the hot, lighted rooms down below to be merely the scene for a political crisis would appear once more as a thin egg-shell moving rapidly through an immense darkness over an element in which men cannot live' (Lewis 1966: 59 f.). Lewis, though he has been falsely accused of misrepresenting Stapledon, here speaks with a Stapledonian voice. Like Stapledon's bird-man, Lewis's Ransom (in *Out of the Silent Planet*) can accept even his own death if it takes place in the heavens: his earth-bound, muddy self feels differently. Once one is in 'one's element' difficulties dissolve: the Lele can work all day long, without hunger, in the forest, but tire quickly in the village, so they say (Tuan 1974: 84, after Douglas).

Or consider Machiavelli's praise of ardent scholarship, a vocation now derided by political 'realists' (a class defined, as Belloc remarks, by their ignorance of the principles on which they act, and the long-term consequences of what they do), social climbers, disgruntled students and other philistines:

On the coming of evening I return to my house and enter my study; and at the door I take off the day's clothing covered with mud and dust . . . and put on garments regal and courtly; and reclothed appropriately, I enter ancient courts of ancient men where, received by them with affection, I feed on that food which only is mine and which I was born for, where I am not ashamed to speak with them and ask them reasons for their actions; and they in their kindness answer me; and for four hours of time I do not feel boredom, I forget every trouble, I do not dread poverty, I am not so frightened by death; I give myself entirely over to them. (Machiavelli to Vettori, 10 Dec. 1513: cited by Hillman 1975: 199)

The last classical philosophers, Stoics, Neoplatonists, and Sceptics alike, would have recognized Olaf Stapledon as one of themselves: humane, ironic, and convinced of his duty both to heart and mind, to eternity and to the present world, to imaginative speculation and to critical care. For Plotinus, the last great classical philosopher, so Armstrong has written, 'philosophical discussion and reflection are not simply means for solving intellectual problems (though they are and must be that). They are also charms for the deliverance of the soul' (1967: 260, after *Ennead* (5. 3. 17). Plotinus looked forward to a great awakening into the living unity-in-diversity of Intellect, described in terms of the interpenetration of a community of living minds.[3] This Intellect has its being and its purpose in contemplation of the rationally incomprehensible One, that from which the universe, itself alive in every part, takes its beginning. The individual soul is 'carried out by the very surge of the wave of Intellect and lifted high by its swell, and suddenly sees without knowing how' (*Ennead* 6. 7 36, 17–19). What it sees is not to be identified with any human love, but no one can ever see it who does not practise virtue and humane benevolence. There is always a distinction, though, between 'higher' and 'lower self'. The Stoic claim that the wise man can positively enjoy being slowly roasted in the bull of Phalaris is merely silly: 'the true self maintains its contemplation of the Good, and so its happiness, unbroken in the midst of torture, but the lower self, which can suffer, really does suffer' (1967: 229). Plotinus, in short, is the source and inspiration of much that is of lasting value in Stapledon. Those who think of him merely as a propagandist for a great science-inspired mythology, neglect the serious philosophical concerns and scholarship that moved him. He did not only look forwards: he was, as any good embodiment of philosophy must be, two-faced also in this. 'For you', the flames tell humankind, 'the golden age is in the future (or so you often like to believe); for us, in the past' (1947: 28). For Stapledon time itself was not all that important, and awakened intellects can greet each other over millenia: the brief golden age of the plant-men, whom I described before, is remembered in the awakening world-spirit, is eternally present to the seeing eye. In their last despair the last men speak of the 'many million, million selves; ephemeridae, each to itself, the universe's one quick point, the crux of all cosmical endeavour. And all defeated! It is forgotten. It leaves only a darkness, deepened by blind recollection of past light. Soon, a greater darkness! Man, a moth sucked into a furnace, vanishes; and then the furnace also, since it is but a spark islanded in the wide, the everlasting darkness. If there is a meaning, it is no human meaning. Yet one thing in all this welter stands apart,

---

[3] God, so Tibetan lamas told Francisco Orazio, 'is the community of all the holy ones' (Kant 1970: 107).

unassailable, fair, the blind recollection of past light' (1963: 605).

Or as a greater poet put it:

O pity and indignation! Manshape, that shone
sheer off, disseveral, a star, death blots black out; nor mark
is any of him at all so stark
but vastness blurs and time beats level. Enough! the Resurrection,
a heart's clarion! Away, grief's gasping, joyless days, dejection.

(Hopkins, 1970: 105)

But that is another story.

Spiritual Exercises

Stapledon was conscious of the spirit in him, with whatever careful irony he presented its demands and failures, and gives some sketchy account of the techniques of mind-control and temperate action that are required—traditionally—of those who would climb higher in the world. It is here that most moderns take leave of tradition. The whole point of 'objective' science is that it makes no difference to the experimental results whether the experimenter is honest, temperate, loving, or courageous. Technology is a device to give us all advantages that were once promised to moral and spiritual athletes. Once upon a time would-be shamans had to learn to preserve their body-heat in freezing waters: now we wear heated suits. Once those who would bring the gods' commands before us had to demonstrate their hardihood, their incorruptibility. Now they need only demonstrate their cleverness, for 'science' has nothing to do with morals. Some scientists continue to claim at least some virtues, of welcoming reasoned criticism and not distorting their results. But anyone who has had occasion to offer such criticisms is all too aware that scientists no more like to have their life-work questioned than the rest of us. Scientists emphatically do not welcome criticism, when it touches on what matters most to them. Science as an institution still survives because professional competition and mutual back-biting serves to ensure that quite a lot of theories are, however painfully, severely questioned—but the institutions that go to make up the invisible colleges also act to divert or conceal criticism when it goes 'too far'.

So modern science is to be distinguished from ancient science by the absence of any internal constraints upon the investigator? Modern scientists are to be governed only by the shifting standards of the colleges, and need not practice any special virtue? There are at least two responses to be made. First, that would-be scientists are in fact required to adopt a certain character approved by their peers. Second, that the ancient virtues, after all, allow a better route.

That scientists are required to adopt a certain character: to achieve the high social and sacred status indicated by 'scientist' the young must practise 'objectivity' and 'controlled scepticism'. Objectivity requires that they empty the world of all personal and emotional affect, that they should not consider what the purpose or goal of any motion is. This attitude can be induced fairly easily in the physical sciences, but only with difficulty in the biological. Controlled scepticism—which is almost wholly uncritical of the preferred methodology of contemporary science—demands that the initiate put on one side all identifiably 'traditional' glosses on the world. In extreme cases this issues in the wilfully ignorant claim that nothing written before the middle nineteenth century can now be worth reading. Alongside these primary demands the initiate is introduced to special ways of seeing that cannot be fully formalized. Learning to see the right shapes in X-ray photographs, as Polanyi has pointed out, is a skill acquired through a long apprenticeship that requires the initiate to 'worship' her guru quite as unconditionally as any ancient apprentice.

Modern science does impose constraints on its initiates, and not always very admirable ones. We cannot so easily distinguish cleverness and moral character, nor claim that a 'good scientist' might have any kind of moral defect. Being a good scientist positively requires one to have some real or supposed virtues. It is unfortunate—to say the least—that some scientists imagine that they can be good scientists without being good citizens or good people, that the professional demands of science are always to be obeyed whatever the human cost. But ancient science also made demands upon its votaries, and sometimes reached past 'merely' human virtue: to free oneself of merely accidental affections, local loyalties, and see things 'straight' required a dedication that would often look like treachery (as poor Cass found the flames). So what is the 'better route' of ancient scientific virtue? What must we become if we are to see things straight and see them whole?

At the very least we need—at first—to struggle against our dreams and wishes. It is often remarked in modern psychology text-books that 'introspection' is a profoundly unreliable method of discovering even what we ourselves think and feel. We are not very good at identifying our own thoughts and feelings and motivations. That is indeed one good reason to turn aside to merely 'external' descriptions of what people do and mean. Public descriptions can be refined and checked: private ones can only be distrusted. Again: it is easily seen that we do not really 'own' the thoughts we say we have. A simple exercise demonstrates a point to which I shall return in later chapters: put this book down, close your eyes, and think simply of a silver unicorn rampant against a blood-red field for the space of thirty seconds.

The point of the exercise, of course, is to reveal how many thoughts and images creep round and about that flickering unicorn, without our conscious guidance. Our thoughts are so far 'not our own' that we cannot easily control them, nor—often—even notice what they were. Can you—honestly—reconstruct the last few minutes' thoughts, and be confident that that was all you thought? 'Whence came the soul, whither will it go, how long will it be our mate and comrade? Can we tell its essential nature? . . . Even now in this life, we are the ruled rather than the rulers, known rather than knowing. . . . Is my mind my own possession? That parent of false conjectures, that purveyor of delusion, the delirious, the fatuous, and in frenzy or senility proved to be the very negation of mind' (Philo, *On Cherubim*, 114 f.: 1929: ii. 77).

Does this signify that introspection, after all, is vain? Why should it? I might as well conclude that no one ever ran a mile in under four minutes, or jumped more than fifteen feet, merely because I cannot. Consider the classicist who charged panting down to Marathon and thence concluded that the Athenians would have no more felt like fighting than he did. Just possibly they were fitter, and better motivated, than he was. Just possibly, and very probably, the shamans, yogis, ascetics of our past are better witnesses to the mind's mountains than we indolent and cowardly rabble can conceive (see Hayward 1987). Only those who have once resisted the tide know how strong it is, or can discriminate its currents. Why should we expect it to be any easier to see what lies 'within' than to see, with understanding, what is without?

3

Destiny and the Will

The Form of Anthropos

In the last chapter I observed in passing that the Unmeaning
Void which some think surrounds us is as much a product of
the imagination as any other world, and as little to be feared
or worshipped. Part of our gift, whatever the truth of things in
general may be, is to make a drama or vision even of what
gives us cause to fear. When we speak of Destiny or the Wheel
of Fortune we speak of what moves on its way regardless of
our wishes, turning kings to beggars and untouchables to
brahmins, but we speak of it in terms that already suggest that
Imagination is the king: who makes wheels but us? 'It seems
strange that we should use the wheel to represent an external
compelling power, when we invented the wheel ourselves to
spin our garments and propel our vehicles' (Frye 1947: 246).
Frye's guess that we made wheels before we began to think
about the cosmos (1947: 266) may not be quite true: perhaps
we brought the wheels of heaven to earth as symbols before we
thought to use them, but the symbols were ours to start with
even so. 'When it is revealed to the initiates [in some tribal
ceremony] that the humans themselves are the ones that
perform the dance . . . [they] learn that their persons extend
into the depth, that they themselves are the successors, whom
they used to think of as beings having an existence apart'
(Duerr 1985: 115).

The assumption that men first conceived themselves as persons and
then applied this conception to the gods is arbitrary and artificial.
This assumption presupposes a secular self-understanding of man
which is clearly an achievement of more recent history. It cannot be
projected backward onto preliterate or archaic man. The reality of the
gods was a primary datum of his experience. . . . The notion of the
personal was later transferred to man because man was honored with
a special relation to the gods. (Pannenberg 1969: 57 f.; see also
Hillman 1975: 17)

The image of the Wheel embodies three fears at least: that what occurs is not to be influenced by us, but rolls on regardless of our mortal plans; that even if 'our' action does affect the world, it is not originally ours, that we are bound to the wheel and can think and love only what the wheel requires of us; and that the very same things happen again and again, without hope of novelty or tangential escape: 'the same dull round, even of a universe, would soon become a mill with complicated wheels' (Blake 1966: 97). It is those three fears, and principally the first two, that I discuss in this chapter. In doing so I shall, as on earlier occasions, appeal to the work of poets as well as philosophers or scientists and refer to gods, demons, and fairies without any qualms. Like Kathleen Raine, I believe that 'From the oldest examples of human art we see humankind seeking to express ideas, to discover a mental order; to explore our inner worlds in terms of pantheons of "gods" who personify the qualities of human consciousness, our moods and modes of experience' (Raine 1982: 5). Like her, I have a particular respect for the Olympian pantheon, as 'intellections of great subtlety, related each to certain fields of knowledge'. Like her (and Blake), I mean by 'humankind' or *anthropos* not the hairless primate, the 'worm of sixty winters', but the immaterial, immeasurable sweep of spiritual being. Where I differ from her occasional belief is in doubting that humankind, the biological taxon, is in truth a separate kingdom from animalkind 'as distinct from the animal kingdom as mammals are from rocks'. I cannot make myself believe that chimpanzees are more like protozoa or pebbles than they are like people, however many poets, philosophers, and zoologists unite to tell me so! That humankind is radically different from what even other primates have been conceived to be I do agree: that we were right so to conceive them, I do not. The form of *anthropos* is not identical with the set of hairless primates that we name 'Homo sapiens' (as Raine of course does know). 'The "human", according to tradition, is not, as for our own society, natural man but the archetypal perfect humanity, of whom every average man is a more or less obscured and distorted image' (Raine 1982: 182 ff.; Clark 1983: ch. 2.2). That archetypal humanity, I shall argue in a later volume, is indeed 'that

individual human being who realizes in himself the reality of
the saying that man is created in God's image . . . , being that
heart . . . in which the Reality eternally rediscovers Its
wholeness' (Austin 1980: 35, after Ibn Arabi).

Two things, then, need to be remembered: on the one hand,
I feel no necessity to understand the human mind only in such
terms as might prove acceptable to learned primatologists
infected by materialist prejudice; on the other hand, I do
believe that any adequate account of the human mind must
rest upon, and help towards, an adequate account of mind as
it manifests itself in other primates, mammals, chordates,
'alien monstrosities'. This programmatic utterance may help
to soothe the puzzlement that some of my readers may in the
past have felt: that on the one hand I profess to see no radical
or morally and metaphysically important distinction between
my conspecifics (just as such) and other animals, and on the
other affirm a spiritual dimension to our lives that is not
readily acknowledged in zoological circles.

I also agree with Raine, and seize this occasion to say so,
that the cult of art as 'self-expression' or 'creativity' rests upon
our having forgotten 'that there can be knowledge of the
invisible worlds':

We cannot expect our children, our young poets and painters to
discover for themselves the abiding order of the invisible worlds.
Just as those who study mathematics or chemistry or plant
morphology respond with recognition to what they are taught, so,
far from inhibiting talent and 'creativity', knowledge of higher
things can only awaken a similar response and widen the field of the
individual imagination (Raine 1982: 12)

The damage has not been only to the arts: fashionable claims
that no arguments are more than subjectively convincing, that
it is wrong ever to claim to know better or reason more
weightily than others, have left a generation without intellectual defence against any kind of fanaticism. 'Everybody has a
right to her opinion' is one of those untruisms that darken
counsel.

From which I draw one further moral, and hope to
eliminate one further confusion that may have affected readers
of my earlier work. The moral is the familiar one, that freedom

from the wheel may not always be worth having, and the bare will not worth acclaiming. The confusion to be eliminated is that I have sometimes, for example, supported Feyerabend in his attack on fixed methodologies, and approved the elaboration of maverick and much-maligned hypotheses. But it does not follow that I (or Feyerabend) reject reason: our shared complaint is not against the Divine Intellect and Imagination, but against those who too easily identify that Intellect with the thoughts they think they have learnt from currently fashionable sages, and dismiss the projects and hypotheses of others with ignorant and arrogant disdain. Philosophers who write that such-and-such a theory 'appeals only to the senile' or that something is 'not now an option' betray their calling.

Why is your language to be regarded as fixed and true, and that of your Spanish brother as 'dangerous' and 'wicked'? No one takes hold of the world immediately; between the two there imposes speech, the language of society, the inherited store of concepts and images. . . . It is by the multiplication of ways of talking that we attain the plenitude of plenitudes. (Lacy 1967: 124, after Unamuno)

But neither Unamuno, Feyerabend, J. S. Mill, nor I thereby reject true reason. What matters is the reminder that such reason involves a difficult ascesis, a humble readiness to transcend past limits.

Fatal Determinism and the Witness

So what about the Wheel of Fate and Fortune? Does my choice affect the way things go, or is my destiny already fixed? Consider the following argument, which some have found fallacious but which seems to me entirely apt.

(1) If an event X has occurred it is now impossible (whether logically or merely physically) to bring it about that X did not occur.

(2) For every action Y that I perform now or in the future there is some past event X which is the sufficient cause of my doing it.

(3) So it is now impossible that I not do any of the things that in fact I shall do.

Since some people find this far from obvious, I must spell it
out.[1] If there is some past event X such that my doing Y
follows by law of logic or of nature, then I can only have it in
my power not to do Y if it is in my power to make X not to
have happened. For if it did, and was sufficient of itself to
ensure that I do Y, then my not doing Y is thereby excluded.
No act or apparent act of mine can be avoided if it will have
been caused by some event that is not in my power (or
anyone's) to unmake. What that event may have been hardly
matters: it is quite true, and any sensible determinist would
admit, that I cannot identify any such inexorable causal
chain. There is no would-be cause that cannot in principle be
obviated by extraneous circumstance. But what is that to the
point? All that follows is that, strictly speaking, the one event
that is sufficient cause of any particular happening, including
any human act, is the one first cause of everything that
happens, that at once ensures both the beginning of any
particular causal chain and that no other causal chains will
interfere with it, that no meteorite will crash into me before
what otherwise would have happened does.

A pragmatic response may be that I shall not know what
action will prove to have been ineluctable until it has
happened, until I have done it. But this is simply an evasion: if
there is one wheel that turns, and this person with it, then
indeed

> with earth's first clay they did the last man's knead,
> and then of the last harvest sow'd the seed:
> yea, the first morning of creation wrote
> what the last dawn of reckoning shall read.

> (Fitzgerald, *Rubáiyát*)

Determinism, in brief, must always have a fatalistic twist. It
may seem to me that I have real options, but I cannot—can
I—stand outside the world to choose what world it will have
been from the beginning.

It is open to us to deny the premises of this argument (as,
please notice, I do), to say that there is, after all, no one

---

[1] John Skorupski and John Porter both assisted my formulation of this
puzzle, though neither agrees with my belief that the argument is valid.

sufficient cause of what occurs or none that occurs 'before' its hapless effect, and that 'causal laws' are only statistical records of what actually does. There are regularities but no compelling causes, and my acts here-now have not been foreordained by any past, unalterable event. It is simply a modern superstition to suppose that anything can be 'explained' by reference to 'natural law' (see Drury 1973: xii, after Wittgenstein 1961: 6. 371). Laws of a merely descriptive kind offer no explanation of the events they describe. Nor do the events or entities mentioned in such laws under the label 'causes' actually determine what comes next. This is one of the many points where modernists sometimes seem to suppose that it is a modern, radical discovery of 'science' that 'causes' are no more determinative of 'effects' than vice versa. But is an ancient thesis that the events we call causes are not to the point:

(1)   what does not exist at all cannot be doing anything;
(2)   what is past no longer exists;
(3)   events called 'causes' occur before the supposed effects;
(4)   when the effect occurs the cause does not exist;
(5)   therefore, the cause (so-called) cannot be causing the effect;
(6)   therefore, it is not a cause.

This argument can be rebutted by the mere insistence that what is past does none the less exist, although not 'now'. If that is so, then we would require an extra thesis to refute all causal influence of past event, namely the denial of 'action at a distance'. Nothing can have an effect at a time and place where it does not exist; what is past does not exist at the same time as the supposed effect; therefore the supposed cause cannot act at the same time as the supposed effect, and therefore is not its cause.

In brief: all that could cause an event X would be something present at that time and place, which is none the less distinguishable from event X (since no such event can cause itself), and which is also the cause of all other events at this or any other time (since there would otherwise be competing causes which could not be guaranteed to agree, such that

events were—in effect—chance by-products of no coherent
system). All that can cause anything, at any moment, is what
we once called God. The argument appears, apparently quite
independently, in Ibn Arabi (1980) and Jonathan Edwards
(see Cherry 1980: 47 f.).

But is God's determining will the only causal element at
work? It is even possible to wonder, after all, whether it may
not be my act that selects the universe I then prove to have
inhabited—though 'my act', in such a (Kantian?) metaphysic,
seems to be something outside time or history (see Plotinus,
Ennead 5. 1. 4, 14–26). Nagel reports (in a book review,
without further detail) that it has been discovered that brain
potential peaks before a decision is consciously taken: does it
follow that the 'decision' was epiphenomenal, or that decisions
fix the past? If we do not deny the premises, a certain
detachment even from what had been our chosen acts appears
inevitable.

We can add a further question: are the laws of destiny
merely natural or moral? Donagan has suggested that it is a
necessary feature of a world in which there are to be moral
agents at all that it be 'a system of nature in which events
occur according to morally neutral laws [and not, for
example, the law of *karma*]' (Donagan 1977: 35). If everything
that happened were immediately and obviously deserved, how
could anyone even succeed in doing wrong? How could I be
doing wrong in battering you to death if that is exactly what
you deserve? But why do you deserve it, and for what wrong
action? Only a bare intention could be the warrant for
punishment or reward, since the actual realization of an
intention would be an event in the world that could only have
happened if it were correct. Consider the Hindu fable of the
sacrificial priest who was suddenly addressed by the goat he
was about to kill: the transmigrating spirit that then animated
the goat had suddenly recalled why it was suffering so, that it
was about to die the last death it had earned by its sacrificial
killings in an earlier life, and felt compassion for the priest
who was now heading for a similar future. The priest
repented, and the goat accordingly broke its neck 'by
accident' a day or two later. The goat's death was inevitable,
but not necessarily the volition by which it looked like coming,

and which alone was culpable. But how can it be culpable to intend to bring about what must and ought to be brought about in any case?

And why, in any case, do we except 'intentions' from the rule that every event is called for by the laws of justice? Why is not a particular intention an event? It is only possible for there to be morally assessible acts and agents if what actually happens at some level or other is not always what ought to happen. It follows that some indefinable amount of what occurs in such a universe ought not to occur, and does not occur because of morally neutral principles.

The system of morally neutral law which we abstract from lived experience, and extrapolate to guide our imagination of what is not here-now, is just what we would expect if there were to be any finite moral agencies. It does not follow, of course, that nothing of what happens is deserved or morally appropriate. We may legitimately understand some happenings as just rewards for sin, even if we would be very unwise to identify particular sins and sinners. But perhaps there are not really any who 'deserve' their fate, and recent human efforts to apportion pains and pleasures in accordance with our sense of justice are a fantasy. Perhaps what happens—and human action so-called must be a part of that—is fixed entirely by the 'law of nature'. Our choices do not influence the outcome, any more than Olympian Zeus.

It is exceedingly difficult to wrap one's mind around this supposition. Indeed, it appears to me to be one of those theories that no one can imaginably apply to her own self. That does not prove it false: any more than the fact that I cannot intelligibly say that everything I seriously believe is false shows that I believe some truths. What cannot be *said* without self-contradiction may still be true. To spell out the story: our predecessors read the lightning as expressive of Zeus' judgement against the powerful, but 'we' recognize that no such meaning need be posited to give an explanation of the event. Lightning just is electrical discharge, and we fully understand it when we see that, things being what they were, the lightning 'must' have struck just then and there, that no one and nothing means a thing by it. Again: our predecessors saw the behaviour of wild beasts as embodying moral purposes, acknowledging authority, forming marital or quasi-marital attachments, dying for their young. 'We' now see those motions as the programmed lurchings of robots built through aeons of Darwinian evolution as devices that scatter bits of DNA more widely. That the animal wanted or intended to do such and such is a cog that does no work: real explanations are to be found in mathematical assessments of survival ratios. Again: even our contemporaries see the behaviour and the speech of people as caused by desires, deliberations, choices of their own. But the 'real' explanation is to be found in neurophysiological analysis of mechanisms that exist as they do on exactly the same terms as those of sea-gulls, ants, amoebas. Intentional explanation of human, and of our own, speech and action is as useless and as superstitious as Olympian Zeus.

Practically no one, you will not be surprised to learn, can actually live by such a story. So radical a refusal of intentional explanation leaves me bemused: I cannot even 'set myself to learn' the language or the mental squint that might permit me to be thus alienated from everything I 'thought' I thought I did. Those philosophers—to whom I shall return—who prefer to agree that intentional description and explanation in both appropriate and sometimes true even though neuro-physiological or naturalistic explanation also is, may be less adventurous, but can at least acknowledge that they are inquiring minds. In doing so, of course, they should also acknowledge that the existence of material regularities in lighting-flash or courtship-behaviour does not of itself prove that intentional description is inappropriate. If I can legitimately see my friend's anger in flushed face, clenched fists, raised voice and blood-pressure (and telling me that I might 'really' be wrong on all such occasions is just silly), even though I also know what other physiological changes preceded and contain those outwards signs, why may I not 'see a god on every wind & a blessing on every blast' (Blake 1966: 291)?

But the attempt to step back from any involvement in the way things go (including the way things go here-now for this body) does have some further merit. Blake's point, in the passage I have just quoted, was, exactly, to warn us against too eager an identification of God's will, and the world's way, with any purposes of ours. We cannot always be sure of the meaning of 'our own' actions and bodily behaviour. After all, we do have the voice of tradition to tell us that 'the self of each of us is not anger or fear or desire just as it is not bits of flesh or fluids either, but is that with which we reason and understand' (Plutarch, *De Facie Lunae* 945^a). Nor was Plutarch therefore committed to the view that it was his true self that 'thought' or 'deliberated' in the way we normally suppose. Remember how little we control our thoughts:

Let the seeker try [not to think] for just five minutes, and he will see what stuff he is made of! He will find that he lives in a clandestine turmoil, an exhausting whirlwind, but never exhausted, where there is room only for his thoughts, his feelings, his impulsions, his reactions, himself, always himself, enormous gnome who obtrudes everywhere, veils everything, hears only himself, knows only himself (if that) and whose perpetual themes, more or less alternating, can give him the illusion of novelty. (Satprem 1968: 32 f.)

Or as a Western writer has it: 'it is a hard matter to bring to a standstill the soul's changing movements. Their irresistible stream is such that we could sooner stem the rush of a torrent, for thoughts after thoughts in countless numbers pour on like a huge breaker and drive and whirl and upset its whole being with their violence. . . . A man's thoughts are sometimes not due to himself but come without his will' (Philo, *Mut.* 239 f.: 1929: v. 265 f.). The exhausting whirlwind of our immediate selfhood follows its own laws, not ours: the witness named in the Upanishads is not identical with the stray thoughts that cross its path any more than with desire or fear or bits of flesh and blood. Detachment from the wheel is not a mythological escape from earthly troubles: it is the awakening of the witness in the discovery that everything that can be said to happen is other than the witness, that the witness does not act nor speak nor think.

Moral Blame and Reasonable Natures

But it remains enormously difficult to live out the conviction (which must itself be only an unowned thought or figment of a

neurophysiological change) that we are not discrete, contributing causes in the world's affairs. That what is, is
determined only 'physically', by the laws of the one Nature, is
not a creed that we as appetitive and thoughtful creatures
can live by. It seems better, or easier, to believe that some of
what occurs is caused by us under just those descriptions that
we give of it, that we can act and often have to endure the
consequences of action, that we are not incapable of turning
our own wheel. But there is a second level of disturbing
thoughts. Perhaps we are the proximate causes of a lot of
things, and perhaps we can select among the options offered
us. We make real choices, after painful thought, and things
would have gone otherwise if we did not. That we behave thus
and so 'because we choose' is an appropriate and often true
judgement, not to be eliminated in any imaginable future
synthesis of psychological knowledge. But the question now
arises: what is choice? Deliberate action is understood in
human terms as 'caused' by an appropriate conjunction of
desire and belief: wishing to be in Cambridge on time and
believing that the train which allows me to be leaves Liverpool
at 9.50, I catch the train. Our actual choices, certainly, are the
product of more complex and less linear systems, but the form
remains. And if my choices are so caused, and my desires and
beliefs themselves arise outwith 'my' choice (or if I only
'chose' to believe that the train left then how lucky I was to get
there!), can I myself be held responsible for what I do? Some
of my beliefs, no doubt, are false, and maybe some of my
desires not such as sane men would admit to having: if
together they cause actions that are not approvable, my
neighbours may restrain me, but can they reasonably 'blame'
me any more than they would blame a madman or a monkey
or a tidal wave? Should they blame me, as a responsible adult,
for not taking steps to correct my errors or re-educate my
passions? Perhaps they should: but maybe I had, for no fault
of my own, no desire or belief that could possibly have had
that effect.

Blaming is a dirty word in left-liberal circles, except when
there is a question of criticizing the police, Americans, or
moralists. I am not myself convinced that those who use such
arguments as I have just been sketching to undermine the

practice have themselves shaken loose of it. Nor am I convinced that 'blaming' is out of place if actions are to be analysed and explained in belief/desire terms (if they are), still less that it is blameworthy. It may now seem that it is unfair to blame people for what they cannot help, and if there is nothing that they are in any position to help, it is therefore unfair to blame them for anything at all. But—leaving aside the obvious wish to *blame* all would-be moralists that is embodied in the preceding argument—the notion that one should only be blamed for what one knowingly does, when one might not have done it, itself rests upon some such distinction between the acts that are genuinely ours and those that are not. The actions of my madness are not 'mine', for 'I' names something other than the disease or demon that possesses me. But if what is causally responsible for the action just is that nature, that complex of desires, beliefs, and temperament that is called 'I', how am I not to blame? The dog or monkey is not, properly speaking, 'blamed' (though what happens to her at our hands may be just as unpleasant), but that is because we do not suppose that dogs or monkeys are likely to be moved by any thought that they have done a wrong. They are not to be distinguished from the natures that they manifest. We do not hold their acts, their characters before them that they may be ashamed—or rather, we do not seriously think that doing this will have, of itself, much use. Making human beings like us ashamed and guilty (or alternatively proud) of what is done is a successful strategy, and not made any less so even if we think that the apparent agent could not, being what she was, do otherwise. By blaming her we give her (and others) reasons, and hence helpful causes, to do otherwise.

If what causes those actions that are reckoned 'mine' is the psychical complex of desire and belief that still remains when once the act is over, then that is what is to blame because that is the proximate cause of the action. We can similarly blame nations, or lesser groups, for what they corporately do, without any belief that nations are 'self-determining' in any other sense than that no one made them do it. The fact, if it is one, that none of these complexes is *causa sui*, seems quite irrelevant. 'The sins of the children visited on the fathers through all generations back to a jealous God!': but what good does that do? If I am not be blamed when that complex is the proximate cause of what was called my act, it can only be because I am not the same thing as the psychical complex of desire and belief that is invoked to 'explain' or to 'make sense of' the action. If I am, then who or what else could sensibly be held at fault?

My suspicion is that this dispute is really theological. Some Abrahamic[2] theologians have held both that human beings are bound by their created nature to sin and that they are therefore damnable. 'Shall the thing formed say to him that formed it, why hast thou made me thus? Hath not the potter power over the clay, of the same lump to make one vessel unto honour and another unto dishonour?' (Paul, Romans 9: 20 f.) 'It is God who showers conceptions (*ennoiai*) on the mind and perceptions (*antilepseis*) on sense, and what comes into being is no gift of any part of ourselves, but all are bestowed by Him, through whom we too have been made' (Philo, *Conf.* 127: 1929: iv. 79). Transcendental 'faults' are not an issue: what counts is the destiny of each created nature. Others have insisted that God could not justly condemn those who could not help themselves, who being what they are for reasons outwith their competence could do no other. I must admit that the thought does have some strength. It does somehow seem very plausible that if there were no genuinely original, self-determining agency, except for God, it would be unfair to blame the finite and determined agents or apparent agents that there are. But of course, if the argument has any reference at all it must refer to God as well: even when that agent acts, what is done is the effect of a complex of desires and beliefs not all of which lie even under His control. God's acts, like ours, are emanations of His nature, and the more immutable because His nature, by hypothesis, is self-sustaining, necessary, and immutable. If we cannot justly be blamed because it was not we that made us out of nothing, then neither can God himself be blamed for blaming us.

Abrahamic theologians have sometimes distanced themselves from ordinarily Platonic ones exactly on this point. Thus

---

[2] A label I have adopted as the name of a religious taxon more nearly of the same rank as Buddhism than is 'Christianity' (Clark 1986b: 16).

Zizioulas, writing from within the Orthodox tradition, rejects the notion that God is determined by an underlying Nature (1985: 40 f.). God's *Arche* is just the Father, the undetermined and creative will, and the unity of His being rests in that. The identity even of a human person rests not upon her nature, but in the indescribable fact of agenthood. Duns Scotus, in a passage that influenced Hopkins: 'Self before nature is no thing as yet but only possible; with the accession of a nature it becomes properly a self, for instance a person' (Hopkins 1959a: 148). Existence precedes essence! As Berkeley said, we have no *idea* of agency or self: such agents are not the same things even as their own ideas, and we know of ourselves only through our notions of agency and obligation. If we allow the distinction between Will and Nature, and concede to God a vaster omnipotence even than most scholastics did, we can rightly hold the Father to be the uncaused cause of all our possibilities. But in so doing we concede the possibility that He has caused us to exist as similarly (though not of course identically) undetermined wills. Our actions, to be understood as actions, must have a certain form, but to be genuinely ours they must be chosen out of many equal possibilities. When we choose we conclude an argument, but nothing compels or causes us to assent to any argument. That we have reason, or even good reason to do so, does not end the matter. 'Although the force of rational love is irresistible, the power of choice is not swamped by it; it rides the flood freely' (Devlin, in Hopkins 1959a: 116).

That action or assent to argument is volitional, and that nothing is strictly voluntary unless it stems from such *voluntas*, is a doctrine that some philosophers, at least since Ryle, have reckoned obviously wrong. I think Ryle's argument is a very bad one, as I shall explain, but I must confess myself not sure what doctrine of the Will makes sense. But as I pointed out in the first volume, my incomprehension is no final test of truth, and when a doctrine is sufficiently attested by my betters I am often obliged to yield to it. When a child is taught words of welcome, 'the child does not understand the words it says by rote, does not know their meaning, yet what they mean it means. The parents understand what they do not say, the child says what it does not understand, but both child and parents mean the welcome' (Hopkins 1959a: 157). What is wrong with admitting that something one does not quite understand must still be true? Even philosophical debate is not all-important. What academic can read Milton's description without a qualm?

> Others apart sat on a Hill retir'd
> in thoughts more elevate, and reasn'd high
> of Providence, Foreknowledge, Will and Fate,
> fixt Fate, free will, foreknowledge absolute,
> and found no end in wand'ring mazes lost.
> Of good and evil much they argu'd then,
> of happiness and final misery,
> passion and apathy, glory and shame,
> vain wisdom all and false Philosophy.
>
> (*Paradise Lost*, 2. 557–65)

Those 'others', remember, are fallen angels wasting time in Pandemonium.

And what was wrong with Ryle's argument? The theory he opposed was that a strictly voluntary act was one caused by the agent's own volition. This, he suggested, must result in a vicious regress: was that volition itself voluntary or not? If it was it must have been preceded by an infinite array of 'acts of volition'; if it was not how could it transmit voluntariness to more public acts? I am baffled that anyone should have found this convincing, and here I am disinclined to yield to my betters. Who said volitions were acts? Or anything but just another name for the agent herself, her will? But suppose there are such mental acts: why is it assumed that they are only 'voluntary' if preceded by another act? One might as well suggest that the presence of water could not be the cause of something's being wet on the grounds that there must then be an infinite array of meta-waters to explain why water itself was wet. Water is present in itself, and so is wet; a volition is essentially voluntary, and transmits its voluntariness to what it causes. By assenting, or 'putting one's will in it', one accepts responsibility for what occurs, and is the cause of it, within a universe that has allowed the opportunity. Mere physical motions are not essentially voluntary, and there is even a class of sort-of-acts that are not; the act of assenting is axiomatically an act of assent, whether to an intellectual argument or to a practical option.

Providence and Human Agency

Suppose that we are, as we think ourselves, free agents in a world we did not make, a world where what occurs is only what is allowed by universal law, but not what is required. Suppose, as theists at least must reckon, what occurs is always in some sense an act of God. What is the relation between my agency and His? How exactly can we be co-workers with Omnipotence, especially when what we do is evil and what He does is axiomatically good? How exactly can we even say that it is right—and such as the Divine Creator could require—that we are agents, quasi-independent wills? After all, the object of the religious exercise is to submerge our will in His: in His will is our peace. The Fall, however fortunate, was constituted by the bid to 'stand apart', to be a 'self-owner' (Plotinus, *Ennead*, 4. 8 4 f.)—or in a later theologian's phrase, to be an 'independent creator of religious and other value' (whatever quite that means; see Clark 1988b). How can we simultaneously be such agents, and be so ruled by the One Will as to will what He does? How, conversely, can we will what apparently He does and not be willing such iniquity as He must be supposed to forbid?

Vernon White's excellent and unjustly neglected piece of philosophical theology, *The Fall of a Sparrow* (1985), gives the groundwork for a bearable analysis. When a wicked act is done, it is part of the world's fabric and there seems no escape from the conclusion that God wills it too. 'Everything that happens is a sacrament of God's will' (Cardenal 1974: 105)—which is to say, an outward and visible sign of an inward and spiritual grace.

Divine Providence is not a disturbing influence, an anomaly in the ordering the world; it is itself the order of the world, or rather it is the regulating principle of this universe. It is eternal Wisdom, unique, spread across the whole universe in a sovereign network of relations. (Weil 1987: 272)

But we must be careful not to end in praising Stapledon's Starmaker, to whom the god of Stapledon's own real devotion offered a magisterial and unanswerable rebuke (1954: 8):

Were the masters of Buchenwald my ministers? Did I, for my poetry's perfection, hunt down negroes for slaves and pack them in the slave-ships? Is all the frustration and agony of all the worlds in all the aeons mere imagery for my poetry?

One of the strongest emotional arguments for atheism, even if it can hardly be expressed in rational form without absurdity, is that the very thought that someone might have intended the world's agonies goes far to making them quite unbearable. 'Only ill will maddens us', according to Rousseau. What we can endure as accident arouses an immortal rage if it was meant—and the Creator, if he intended Buchenwald, must have intended just that furious response as well.

> What meaneth Nature by these diverse laws?
> Passion and Reason self-division cause.
> Is it the mark or majesty of Power
> to make offences that it may forgive?
> Nature herself doth her own self deflower,
> to hate those errors she herself doth give.
>
> (Fulke Greville, 'Mustapha': Gardner 1972: 118)

White's conclusion is that the One Will must be supposed to intend what happens under some description, but not under the same description as we do. Nor can He intend our willing evil, even though what we succeed in doing, by His collaboration and support, is to be accounted good under the description that He wills. So Berkeley:

We ought not to repine at the dispensations of providence, or charge God foolishly. I say it becomes us with thankfulness to use the good things we receive at the hand of God, and patiently to abide the evil, which when thoroughly considered and understood may perhaps appear to be good, it being no sure sign that a thing is good, because we desire, or evil, because we are displeased with it. (1948: vii. 134)

Berkeley's problem, and ours, is not only the emotional or ethical one of how to see as God sees and 'bless what there is for being'. The question, as before, is this: what is the relation of our agency to God's? If we were only and forever spectators of reality we would simply have to enjoy what happened: as it is, we have the overwhelming sense of contributing to it, and get our very concept of causation from the experience of agency. But how can we be truly said to cause or affect a thing if it is God's volition that determines every effect? Our sense of agency seems in danger of dissolving into illusion. As Plotinus pointed out, if the world were a unity, a fixed whole, in the sense that the Stoics supposed, 'we are no We' (*Ennead*, 3. 1. 4, 21 ff.). What can I directly do? There are moderns who imagine that to lift my arm I only have to lift it, as if the mere attempt were necessarily effective. It should be clear that, as Geach has pointed out apropos of Nebuchadnezzar (1969: 126 f.), one cannot reach the end of one blasphemous sentence without the co-operation of the created universe and God's sustaining Will (see Weil 1987: 276).[3] In so far as God has allowed me any will at all—which is to say, in so far as I myself exist at all—my will directly affects only my own personal world. That is one reason among many why theists must be Berkeleians: every created thing must stand to God in much the same relationship as items of my personal subjectivity stand to me. Or rather, they stand to God as I can conceive such items to stand to me: for, as I have pointed out already, even my personal subjectivity is an exhausting and uncontrolled whirlwind of thoughts, desires, and fancies.

Or is that idealized comparison an error? If it is beyond our reach to see the universe as informed by one consistent plan, might we not more plausibly conceive that the Divine Imagination—so far as we can picture it to ourselves—is as murky and confused as ours? The merit of polytheism as a working creed is that it takes the plurality of plans and values and discrepant strategies with proper seriousness. That there is One Will overall, One intellectual Form to which all things must move, may also be a necessary creed, but it is certainly a lot easier to conceive the universe as the arena of competing deities. We do not actually possess one single viewpoint on creation that makes sense of everything: we live within

---

[3] That our sanity, as Drury remarks (1973: 134), 'is at the mercy of a molecule' merely confirms what the god-fearing always knew.

indefinitely many provinces of meaning, and employ indefinitely many modes of explanation. If it is absurd to think that everything can—in this life, at least—be incorporated in a single theory, who not accept that our best model of the Divine is about as plural as our shifting selves?

Instead of one wheel, we are faced by many: wheels within wheels, and each is full of eyes. Maybe as we refine our own attention, our own shadow-worlds, we see how the One World might stand behind the manifold perspectives, but would still be rash to say that we have even the end of that golden string that one day leads us in to Heaven's Gate. One of the oldest of our images is that there is real War in Heaven. But Neoplatonic polytheism is a dangerous creed: perhaps, for all monotheism's perils, we should still insist that there is One God only as there is also, in the end, just One World only. I do not seriously wish to advocate polytheism: on the contrary, I want to point people on past those modernist imaginings that amount to polytheism to a renewed, monotheistic commitment. But the reminder of what our ordinary selves are like may help to answer the question I have posed.

That question, remember, was: how can a happening be simultaneously the effect of my volition (and therefore my act, for which I thereby admit responsibility and for which I am judged), and also the effect of the One God's volition? Must God be one agent among many who might defy Him, or does His agency absorb all others, so that our sense of acting is a mere illusion? Who killed the butler? Was it Joe or Jane? Or maybe Joe poisoned the tea, and Jane poured it out (both knowingly)? Or Jane at least knew just what Joe had done, and encouraged the butler to drink deep? Could Jane then plead that Joe alone was blameable? Jane did not only make it possible for Joe to kill, by standing aside or carefully looking away (which must be bad enough): Joe could not have done so without Jane's constant help and care. Can Jane now plead that she did not intend the death? Especially if Jane herself is known to have killed housemaid, stable lad, and all without involving Joe.

God takes [the Devil] by the hand and says: 'Devil, you are indeed a murderer and a wicked spirit, but I will use you for my purposes;

you shall be only my pruning-knife, and the world and all that
depends on you shall be my manure-heap for my beloved vineyard'.
(Luther: cited by Brown 1968: 201)

Such anecdotes do show that there is nothing impossibly odd
about collaborative enterprises, even ones when Joe, as it
were, does not quite realize how much help he has had. Both
Joe and Jane must share the guilt; both killed. But Jane had
a right to kill, we might suppose: Jane did, but Joe did not,
and so Jane acted within her rights, and Joe's a criminal.
Perhaps, but how else should Jane appoint an agent than by
so clearly allowing and abetting what Joe did? How else did
God appoint Cyrus the Persian as Messiah than by allowing
him the victory? If Jane killed rightly, and abetted Joe, was
she not thereby licensing Joe's killing? Perhaps Joe did not
realize the case: his sin is not the killing, but the imagining
that he did not need Jane's permission. Nothing that God
permits and abets, by this analogy, can be a crime: the only
sin is to imagine oneself as God, self-licensed to attempt just
what one chooses. The Assyrians do God's will in punishing
Israel, but they too will be punished for their intent to wipe
out nation after nation (Eller 1973: 78, after Isaiah 10: 5–13).
Those who are conscious of their dependency, and try
with all their strength to do what they are ready to see fail
by God's command, therefore commit no sin. Success
vindicates our plans—though it is perhaps not easy to detect
success.

Therefore do all your acts as worship: God's will is always
done, and no one dies whose death was not intended.

But once again the mere imagining or intending that we are
self-owners is itself an event that the One God permits, aids,
and abets. The 'sin' is itself a part of 'the infinite path Three-
Personed substance weaves'. Joe's killing of the butler as a
vengeful or a greedy act is what is apparently endorsed, not
only the butler's death—unless it is supposed that only the
first wheel of physical event is God-sponsored or controlled,
and the epicyclic wheels of personal motivation are beyond
God's reach. But once admit that God's grace can change my
motives and renew my being, His not doing so now but rather
supporting me from one second to the next in all my rebellious

fervour amounts to licensing that very rebellion. And God, in any case, did not only 'allow' Pharaoh to resist, but actually hardened Pharaoh's heart, for His own purposes. Job is vindicated not because he patiently endured what God had sent, but because he carried his insistent questioning before the Lord: the answer he gets is that the Lord gives everything its season, whether it be antelope or lion, coney or hippopotamus . . . or Satan (see Clark 1986b: 151).

Maybe we should indeed stop there: nothing I have said was intended to subvert our necessary 'consent to Being' or lend any credence to a fantastical revolt against Omnipotence. If it is possible to stand over against the Lord so far as to defy Him, there must be many agents and the Lord not responsible for all that happens; if, contrariwise. He is, then true rebellion cannot even be imagined. But one further turn is possible. Suppose we use an internal rather than external model, and consider the ways in which 'one act' might still be multiple, without involving us in stories about Joe and Jane. Perhaps the relation of God and finite agent is not quite like that of Joe and Jane, even if Jane is seen as an accessory before, during, and after the fact (for her own purposes). It is better to recall the essential multiplicity of human agency, and so of the inner realms. When Homer attributes spiteful or skilful or other action to a god, he does not imply that a named human person should not also bear the blame. 'Aphrodite did it' does not mean that Helen did not. When 'I' act, the truth is that indefinitely many spirits move toward completion, and what we ordinarily conceive as a single action has multiple significance.

The Eternal Return

And does the wheel come round again, so that, as Marcus Aurelius supposed, a man of 40 might have seen every sort of thing the universe contains? The round world's imagined corners are Spring, Summer, Autumn, Winter, and nothing in the House of Time is really new.

> Another Troy must rise and set,
> another lineage feed the crow,
> Another Argo's pointed prow
> drive to a flashier bauble yet.
>
> (Yeats 1950: 244)

The destiny in which we are embedded is a finite world, however vast.

'The same thing's happening over and over again' is a feature of the passing of time as it is for us: just as there are no boundaries within a value-free nature, so there are no seasonal repetitions. Seasons, like species, are features of a humanly conceived world. Winter is as astrological a concept as the House of Sagittarius. But the thought of such seasonal variation and repetition is at least very useful when we consider plant-life or animal breeding patterns. The historiographical question is whether there are similar seasons to be detected in the affairs of humankind. Do nations or civilizations thrive and decay in something like the way we think that other creatures do?

> Cities and thrones and powers
> stand in time's eye
> almost as long as flowers,
> which daily die:
> but as new buds put forth
> to glad new men,
> out of the spent and unconsidered earth
> the cities rise again.
>
> (Kipling 1927: 479)

That notion of Destiny is both disheartening and consoling: each age, nation, cultural form has its own period and peak. 'In the sea a wave mounts higher and higher; but at a certain point, where there is none the less only space, it is arrested and forced to redescend' (Weil 1987: 274). All mortal shapes must perish, no matter what we individual mortals do; but also, all mortal shapes strive after immortality according to their kind, and new generations rise to repeat the story. Even those of us who know a little too much history to be quite convinced by Spengler's parallels between successive ages of distinct cultures, each with its governing mythos and creative power, its hardening arteries and long brutalization into empire, enforced by militarists on fellahin, can feel a quaint attraction in the idea. We would like to think that history is not just one 'damned thing after another' even if, like other ill-written tragedies, it lacks a single beginning, middle, and end. In Spenglerian terms each governing idea is finite and exhausts itself, so that no further advance can be made without a radical shift of paradigm, myth, methodology. The very idea (which some still optimistically aver) that we have almost achieved a complete synthesis of knowledge is a sign that 'our' Western civilization is almost over. The life of the race, the underlying nature, lies in its capacity to think new thoughts, create new images for a millenial refinement. Or rather, to rediscover the 'burl of being', the secret rhizome from which new growth springs.

4

Beasts and Angels

Whether or not there really are many centres of agency, many
individual wills that somehow co-operate with agencies within
and outside the organisms that we imagine ourselves to be,
our actual experience is of action. We experience ourselves as
pilots of a ship, or rulers of a squabbling horde of fantasies, or
animal tamers. Whether the image is of Heracles, perfecting
his laborious life by the long struggle with the Nemeian Lion,
or the ox-herd of the Chinese painting who hunts down and
rides home the ox of his mind, we are conscious of the effort
that goes into organizing ourselves.

> Just as a man would tie to a post
> a calf that should be tamed,
> even so here should one tie one's own mind
> tight to the object of mindfulness.
>
> (Cited by Rahula 1978: 16)

Maybe the truly virtuous do not any longer experience right
action as an effort, and have no rebellious parts: few of us
possess true virtue. There is a curious, and unFreudian,
perversion of Freud's theory to the effect that 'virtuous' people
do not suppress their impulses, nor allow 'moralistic' qualms
to stand in the way of 'what makes life worth living', what
they 'really' want to do. Malicious gossip, patronizing
moralism, and masochistic self-abasement are either exempted
from this blanket approval of 'the natural man', on the ground
that they cannot 'really' be 'natural', or else—or simultaneously—indulged to the full by the very people who
announce their moralistic disapproval of all moralizing.
Blake's mysterious comment that 'those who restrain desire
do so because theirs is weak enough to be restrained' (Blake

1966: 149) was not a libertine's excuse for acting out his feeble fancies. Our error is not that we 'give in to our desires', but that we are too easily satisfied. 'The desire of Man being Infinite, the possession is Infinite & himself Infinite' (Blake 1966: 97): but we here-now are not—quite—*Man*.

There are many springs of 'voluntary action', broadly so called, in a single human organism. We do some things 'out of desire' even when we do not, or would not seriously, 'choose' to do them, but those desirous or indulgent acts are still, in some ways, 'ours', even if we afterwards, or simultaneously, disown them. Rare is the person who has not sometimes felt quite out of control, a horrified spectator of her own abominable behaviour. The lion of one's heart is in a huff, or the squamous and many-headed monster that Plato identified with lust—but not with *Eros* himself—is grabbing all it can while conscience or intellect is in a daze. My own suspicion is that Plato's account misleads a little: some actions that our 'central self' disowns or cannot understand stem not from Lust, nor even from Self-reflective Pride or Shame—which is what *thumos* amounts to—but from illicit curiosity. What would it be like to be the sort of person who does that sort of thing, and not the boring selfhood that is shrieking in the rear? That, perhaps, is part of the reason why some later commentators made a distinction between intellect and conscience, that there are errors of the intellect as well as of bodily desire and *thumos*. Jerome identifies four parts of the human soul, not the Platonic three: *synteresis*, symbolized by the eagle of Ezekiel's vision, is not mixed up with the other three, but corrects them when they go wrong (Jerome in Ezekiel 1: 7: Potts 1980: 79 f.). I shall have more to say in a later chapter about Conscience as a controlling *daimon*. In this, I am chiefly concerned with the experience of moral struggle, and with the endemic tendency to identify those aspects of our selfhood that we struggle against with animals.

Well, when do we act like sheep? When we act for the sake of the belly, or of our sex-organs, or at random, or in a filthy fashion, or without due consideration. When we act pugnaciously, and injuriously, and angrily, and rudely, to what level have we degenerated? To the level of the wild beasts. (Epictetus, *Discourses*, 2. 9. 2)

The 'beast within' is not necessarily unsocial: when crowds 'behave like animals', as judges and reporters say, it is because their individual selfhoods and discrimination are submerged in what amounts to a 'hive mind'. People abandon duties of careful thought or courtesy, and disclaim the very acts that they knowingly perform, not only because of individual fear, lust, or anger (emotions that are or would be felt with the same strength even if the person involved were all alone), but because of a highly social, integrative spirit. Hatred, panic fear, bellicosity, and punitive self-righteousness may all be identified with 'inner beasts' that are also public, intersubjective realities. Nor is the 'beast', as we conceive it, always a thing of warm emotion. 'Beastly' behaviour may be stereotypic, 'ritualized', indifferent to the further consequences or the support of others.

The claim that it was not 'I' that acted, but my bestial self, may sometimes be a simple lie. People do do dreadful things, even things that they themselves think or will think dreadful, for humanly comprehensible reasons. It might have been useful, before the act, to think of its doing as something that stemmed from a bestial or diabolic source: often the only thing to do with a temptation is to order it away—or, since we are not the type that devils willingly obey, make some appeal to higher authority (on which more below). But once we have consented to it, the act is ours. The man who rapes his daughter or breaks his child's arm 'to teach his wife a lesson' cannot plead that the act, though voluntary, was not really his. He may, later on, pretend to himself and others that the aberration did not reveal his 'real self', that it was a dark alien that acted in his place. He may genuinely, and absurdly, imagine that the act he did was at least not quite as bad as it would have been if it were directed solely at his own sex-satisfaction, or solely to his child's hurt. What he cannot sensibly claim is that he was 'behaving like an animal'. If that expression means anything it presumably conveys that someone was acting out a stereotypic behaviour pattern or giving rein to casual emotion, without regard to consequences or the acknowledged opinion of others.

That our chief political and personal problem is to control our beastly inclinations is an ancient theory, which has seriously affected our relationships with those humans and non-humans whom we perceive as relatively 'unhuman', undomesticated, barbarous, or wild. That ancient theory is founded not on serious observation of non-human animals, but on ideological needs:[1] Hesiod's notorious dictum that beasts devour each other, living without *dike*, which is the gift of Zeus to men (*Works and Days*, 275 ff.), a sense of decency and place, which is not well captured by any talk of abstract justice. We must not live like animals, but by a higher law; animals, to give us a proper foil, must be supposed to live as we ought not, but as we would if civil society failed. Animals enter political philosophy not only as the concrete dogs, cats, pigs, horses, cattle with whom we share our lives, and the equally concrete wolves, lions, snakes, and bears that once we feared, but also as symbols of such forms of life as we free, adult, male members of society may wish to exclude, idealize, or tame. It is through our fleshy kinship with the animals that we may grow like wolves, faithless, treacherous, and hurtful, or like lions, or foxes (Epictetus, *Discourses* 1. 3. 7). Bad men, so Aristotle said (*Nicomachean Ethics* 7, 1150[a]3) are worse than any beasts, but that is only because they choose their bestiality: what they choose is the life beasts live without realizing it. Civil, civilized existence rescues us from falling prey to real animals, and our own 'animal nature'. Epictetus, and others, held that our true human nature, that by which we could claim kinship with the gods, with God, was best revealed by distance from the 'animal'. Animals did not need to understand or discriminate: men are the spectators and interpreters (Epictetus, *Discourses* 1. 6. 18 f.). Others held that it was only custom, *nomos*, that protected us: by nature we would be what the beasts supposedly are. Some, like Plato's Callicles, preferred what they believed to be the natural life, the perpetual demand for more and better pleasures. Others, like Plutarch (*Gryllus* 987[b]), wondered if it was custom that perverted natural virtue, the calm recognition of necessity. Attitudes varied, but there was considerable agreement about

[1] Some of the following material was tried out at conferences on ancient political theory in Cambridge and Manchester, and published in Clark 1990*b*.

the way that non-humans lived, the way we would have lived,
or might live still, if civilization failed us.

Dio Chrysostomus records Diogenes' ironic remark on the subject of
Oedipus: 'Oedipus bewails the fact that he is father and brother to
his children and husband and son to his wife but that is something
that neither cocks nor dogs nor birds complain about', for among
those creatures there are no such things as brothers, fathers,
husbands, sons or wives. Like isolated pieces in a game of draughts
they live without rules, knowing neither difference nor equality, in
the confusion of anomia. (Vernant and Vidal-Naquet 1981: 118
n. 23)

In speaking as he does Diogenes stood in a long tradition. Till
Prometheus took a hand our ancestors 'had eyes but saw to no
purpose, heard but took no heed: like dream-shapes they lived
their long lives in utter confusion' (Aeschylus, *Prometheus*
440 f.). It was a 'mixed up and bestial existence' that some
god saved us from, giving us understanding, language,
agriculture, shelter, sea-voyages, and trade and augury
(Euripides, *Supplices*, 201 ff.). Before that day, our ancestors
lived, as the further barbarians do now, by sense and not
intelligence (Aristotle, *Nicomachean Ethics* 7, 1149^a 10). If it was
a Golden Age, when death and senility were unknown, it was
only because no one lived to be senile, and no one knew what
death was (Tzetzes: Cole 1967: 10). Hephaistos and Athene
established us in houses, where before we had lived like
beasts, wandering the hills like deer, in tattered clothes
(*Homeric Hymn* 10; Theognis 55–6). Humans alone have
households; others live promiscuously (Aristotle, *Eudemian
Ethics* 7, 1142^a 23). It is because we have acquired a sense of
civil distinctions, shame, respect, that we can both maintain a
civil peace among ourselves and be masters of wild nature.
Alternatively, by Diogenes' transvaluation of the coinage, it is
because we make unreal distinctions, and live by customary
rules, that we live 'unnatural' lives. Diogenes' abandonment
of civil life was perhaps only partial: he lived a 'dog's life'—
but other and more fearful outlaws lived as wolves (consider
the cannibals of Zeus Lykaios) or lived as the Greeks thought
wolves lived.

Some god gave understanding, language, agriculture, sea-
faring, trade, and augury, and so brought our ancestors'

scattered, confused, and bestial existence to an end. Previously, they had been at the mercy of the wild beasts (Dicaearchus fr. 67: Cicero, *De Officiis* 2. 5), beings whose way it is to prevail over each other by violence. Their union, of the weak against the strong, brought us the art of politics, of which warfare is a part (Plato, *Protagoras* 322 B). Till then, the stronger killed and ate the weaker: but the weak banded together under an animal-sign (Diodorus 1. 90. 1), and now resolve their differences by law (ps—Lysias 2. 18 f.). The war with beasts (and with the human outlaws who make beasts of themselves) is fundamental to human civil order. Without law and order we should all be savages, undiscriminating in our casual affections, violent in our revenges, and philistine in our attitude to art and science alike. Because they thought that we would be like that without the constant presence of the law, generations of Europeans have convinced themselves that non-Europeans actually were like that. So Samuel Johnson: 'Pity is not natural to man. Children are always cruel. Savages are always cruel. Pity is acquired and improved by the cultivation of reason' (Boswell 1953: 309). Again, replying to one who 'expatiated on the happiness of the savage life':

Do not allow yourself to be imposed upon by such a gross absurdity. It is sad stuff; it is brutish. If a bull could speak, he might as well exclaim—Here I am with this cow and this grass; what being can enjoy greater felicity? (Boswell 1953: 521)

'Besides, sir, a savage man and a savage woman meet by chance; and when the man sees another woman that pleases him better, he will leave the first' (Boswell 1953: 474).

Gross men prefer animal pleasure. So there are men who have preferred living among savages. Now what a wretch must he be, who is content with such conversation as can be had among savages! You may remember an officer . . . who had served in America told us of a woman whom they were obliged to bind, in order to get back from savage life (Boswell: 'She must have been an animal, a beast'). Sir, she was a speaking cat. (Boswell 1953: 912)

This dangerous and dreadful nonsense, which treats those of another history and culture as unthinking animals, and denies any right to choose another culture than one's own, has its own mirror image: some, like the Cynics, have always been ready to see the 'natural' life as good, 'free and unrestrained amid the rude magnificence of Nature' (the gentleman whom Johnson mocked as brutish), and identified that with the actual life of particular foreign tribes. Johnson was probably right to insist that, for instance, the Otaheite are 'not in a state of pure nature; for it is plain they broke off from some other people' (Boswell 1953: 757). People found wandering in the forests of the Philippines (as 'The Gentle Tasaday') are only 'primitive survivors from the dawn of humanity' in the eyes of credulous journalists like Nance 1984 (they turn out to have been stooges—and dupes—of the Marcos regime). Archaic Greek thought gives us as good, and as bad, a model for the thought and habits of our first human ancestors.

Where Johnson thought that the Otaheite must simply have forgotten all law and culture, we are readier to agree that they had remodelled them, that there are no tribes of savages as Johnson understood the term. But we retain something of the older view: those who behave like animals, in popular parlance and the lawcourts, are those who have forgotten the restraints of law and culture, and loosed their blind, brute passions. The truth is, of course, that genuinely animal passions are mild by comparison with ours, and the greatest crimes the product of excess, not natural need (Aristotle, *Politics* 2, 1267^a 13). Bad men are worse than beasts. Rage, greed (which includes vulgar curiosity) and fear (which can at a pinch be identified with merely 'animal' impulses) may be the engines that drive our personal lives astray, but no one goes to war to fill his belly or in a fit of bad temper. The more bestial the crime, the greater it is (Aristotle, *Rhetoric* 1, 1375^{a}6) perhaps, but not even wild beasts behave in as 'bestial' a fashion as some humans, and though we may be at war with them (as Isocrates and others have claimed), they have no strategic plans about us. We are warring and contentious animals not because we are like other animals, but because we are rather unlike them. Chimpanzee groups may battle it out with neighbouring groups, but not because they think their neighbours are immoral, and not with any intention of leaving no alien to tell the tale. It is not clear that they are inflicted with any consciousness of sin, or intend some symbolic meaning to their acts. The bestialities that Aristotle mentions—

eating dirt or human embryos (*Nicomachean Ethics* 7, 1148^{b}20 ff.)—are not likely to be simple responses to a vitamin deficient diet or a lack of culinary discrimination: they are cultural and symbolic acts as clearly as Ezekiel's, even if their meanings are such as we abhor. 'In man and other primates', as Cranach remarks, 'a movement is never just a movement. At least partly its identity emerges from its meaning' (Cranach 1979). And what, if anything, cannibalistic chimpanzees may mean, we do not know.

Our political philosophy, all too often, is predicated on the assumption that State Law was and is needed to control the wild, animal passions that would otherwise make life impossible. My own view, described at length in the first volume, is that neither other animals nor our 'uncivilized' selves are as bad as ideologues suppose. Ingrained behaviour patterns, and the power of custom, may keep as much peace as anyone could expect, without invoking Leviathan. Civil war is not a state of nature, but the decay of statism. Nor do I see our main political problem as the need to control 'the beast within': history suggests that idealists, not ordinary sensualists nor even ordinary, muddled human animals, do the most harm. Those who fear the beast hope to establish a rational order of society that all persons may internalize to help control their whims and fancies. Like Plato, they would put our destiny in the hands of experts. Unlike Plato, they seem not to recognize the danger posed by those who think themselves experts, without any epistemic warrant for the claim, nor any evidence of unusual wisdom, courage, temperance, and justice. Those, like myself, who respect the inarticulate and untutored leanings of the human animal enough to doubt the claims of the revisionists, prefer a civil order that restrains idealists— and my shifty self—as well as egoists and knaves.

I myself think the bestiality of 'the beast within' and that of its non-human cousins out there in the world, 'the beast outside', has been much exaggerated. My political conservatism has more links with the anarchist or classical liberal tradition than with the moralizing of fascists and state-socialists. I am, equivalently, more inclined to favour ways of minimizing evil than of maximizing good. Natural parents do not always rear their children well; I think there is good reason to suppose that self-styled experts often rear them worse.[2] But the fact remains that the image of the beast within, and its cousins outside, is endemic. It is not a Western fantasy, as if all other peoples were at ease with their organic natures and the world at large—though that itself is a revealing fantasy. We want to be told that somewhere or other there are people who are not at odds with themselves, that there is a culture which does not create interpersonal or intrapersonal tensions, that the 'natural human' is as simple and straightforward as even Plato would wish. Why else did people accept Mead's fantasies of Samoa so uncritically? That is what perhaps lies behind the assumption made by Hume and others, that Justice is only needed because we live in a world of scarce resources and limited affections: if there were only enough goodies for everyone's wants, and everyone was as fond of any human person as of her child or spouse, we would have no problems. Hume at least remembered that we did not live in that imagined world: some utopians have spoken as if we could, that something called 'Science' would bring the dawn. Spare us from do-gooders who do not realize that people's opinions differ even about what's good for them, that there are real difficulties about ordering even one's own priorities, one's own soul, that advocates of 'universal love' all too often end as murderers. Are all prosperous and affectionate families immunne to moral danger? Would that they were.

> Cruelty has a Human Heart,
> and Jealousy a Human Face;
> Terror the Human Form Divine,
> and Secrecy the Human Dress.
> The Human Dress is forged Iron,
> the Human Form a fiery Forge,
> the Human Face a Furnace seal'd,
> the Human Heart its hungry Gorge.
>
> (Blake 1966: 221)

Other peoples may have other concepts of the People to which they belong, and classify our conspecifics in ways that liberals,

---

[2] I have considered the fate of children at the hands of parents and experts in Clark 1989a.

or any humane Westerners, do not admire. That all and only members of the species *Homo sapiens* deserve our special care is a political doctrine that not every rational person would or must endorse. But wherever we have found those creatures that we recognize as human, having human languages and culture (and who have so far turned out to be our conspecifics, though nothing says they must), they also turn out to make a distinction between 'those like them' and the uncivil others, to whose nature they feel an affinity, and assimilation to which they must, individually and socially, resist. Stories about cannibals and incestuous tribes may sometimes have a residue of fact: but they are mostly told to give some sense of what it is that 'really human' peoples must abjure, even while they admit, through fantasy, that they quite like the idea. Chimpanzees, we may suppose, do not tell stories about how dangerous it would be to be baboons. All human groups, by contrast, seem to be conscious of the fragility of 'human' order, and of the possibilities our souls contain, even if it is not always the same possibilities that most horrify us.

Angels, Devils, and Established Orders

The Beast, in other words, represents to us the overthrow of an established order, within our individual souls and in society. It may make use of 'natural impulses', lust or rage or laziness, but what makes it fearful is the thought that those impulses, and our deliberate choice, might ground a different social and psychic order to which our order would be anathema.

> And (impudent heathen!) They look upon We
> as a quite impossible They!
>
> (Kipling 1927: 710)

The Beast within and the Alien without embody the same fear: that something else is possible, and nothing beyond the barest imaginable 'animal impulses' for food, warmth, safety, sex is necessary.

But why is it possible? And why do we fear the thought? If

chimpanzees do not fear to be baboons, why on earth do humans fantasize about being solitary predators, or herd animals, or cannibalistic and incestuous ogres? A conventional answer, for a hundred years or so, is that in the human species biological evolution has been displaced by cultural. We are born without innate ideas or instincts of a complexity sufficient to ground the behaviour needed to survive. The Lord has not written His laws in our hearts: instead we must learn them, or make up substitutes. We must hammer, burn, and carve those laws into our inheritors. We are born as open-minded apes: and the trouble with an open mind, as someone said, is that people will keep putting things in it—as so they must, if we are to survive at all. Untutored, uncontrolled 'experience' cannot get us anywhere, in epistemology or in politics. All human groups must therefore guide their young, selecting certain possibilities as their guiding themes and demoting others to the underworld. Any of us might have been 'a foreign devil' or an untutored beast, and carry the option with us still. That is one reason why anyone who has explored her self must be profoundly sceptical about the claims of those who would erect any particular social order as the one that 'we' would, in the abstract, choose. Anyone who says that there are rules 'that can be endorsed from all points of view—not only no matter what one's actual condition is, but also no matter what one's actual ideas and values are' (Mackie 1976: 154) is seeking a stability that does not exist, having quite forgotten the actual diversity of ideas and values. All personal and social orders relegate and vilify real possibilities which would, if they were dominant instead, engender other orders.

> Owls—they whinny down the night;
> bats go zigzag by.
> Ambushed in shadow beyond sight
> the outlaws lie.
> Old gods, tamed to silence, there
> in the wet woods they lurk,
> greedy of human stuff to snare
> in nets of murk.
> Look up, else your eye will drown
> in a moving sea of black;

between the tree-tops, upside down,
goes the sky-track.
Look up, else your feet will stray
into that ambuscade
where spider-like they trap their prey
with webs of shade.
For though creeds whirl away in dust,
faith dies and men forget,
these aged gods of power and lust
cling to life yet—
old gods, almost dead, malign,
starving for unpaid dues:
incense and fire, salt, blood and wine,
and a drumming muse,
banished to woods and a sickly moon,
shrunk to mere bogey things,
who spoke with thunder once at noon
to prostrate kings:
with thunder from an open sky
to warrior, virgin, priest,
bowing in fear with dazzled eye
towards the dread East—
proud gods, humbled, sunk so low,
living with ghosts and ghouls,
and ghosts of ghosts and last year's snow
and dead toadstools.

(Graves 1966: 18)

But of course the fact that those old gods still live at all is
evidence that there is an abiding landscape of the soul: the old
actualities are still possibilities. It is even possible for those
disenchanted with the present order to point to the abiding
power of humble and neglected gods.

Only a man harrowing clods
in a slow silent walk
with an old horse that stumbles and nods
half asleep as they stalk.
Only thin smoke without flame
from the heaps of couch-grass;
yet this will go onward the same
though Dynasties pass.
Yonder a maid and her wight

Come whispering by:
war's annals will cloud into night
ere their story die.

(Thomas Hardy, 'In Time of "The
Breaking of Nations" ', Gardner 1972: 771)

We are not really quite such empty tablets at our birth, nor
are our foreign neighbours as opaque to our imaginations as
they would be if they had really begun their own eccentric
story at some arbitrary other point. We have not yet
discovered any speaking peoples whose experience could not
be mapped on ours, nor are each other's dreaded beasts quite
so dissimilar. Even if they were, of course, that would
establish even more strongly what it was that we all had in
common: namely, the predisposition to select, organize, and
polarize. Even to learn 'from experience', which some
theorists have insisted is our chief or only route to knowledge,
requires that we have an inbuilt disposition (simply put) to
repeat the moves that have once been associated with what
(by inbuilt standards) we count success. There can be no
inductive inference, even of the least self-conscious kind,
without a priori warrant—and if we have to admit that much
to be innate, we may as well acknowledge that much more
might be. There is, for all of us, a pattern that controls or seeks
to control our life, and vagrant impulses that are conceived as
enemies of that controlling order. Human experience is of the
contest between Beast and Angel.

Dogmatic monists will resent this claim: dualism, they tell
us, or 'Platonic dualism', arises from a mistaken fear of bodily
appetites, a tendency to misidentify 'oneself' with 'higher'
things. The metaphysical distinction between soul and body,
the inner life and the realm of physics, is a projection of the
moral distinction between spiritual and material value: what
we 'really' are are psycho-physical organisms whose spiritual
needs are inextricably entangled in material ones, and whose
inner life depends on physical well-being. It is a superstition
or a 'category-mistake' to think of 'souls' as 'counter-persons,
duplicate persons, inner persons, possessed of cognitive
faculties, and imprisoned or entombed or tainted by the bodies
that accompany them around' (see Robinson 1970: 25). There

are still old-fashioned people who are inclined to see a difference between the inner self and either the public face with which we greet the world, or the 'clandestine turmoil, the exhausting whirlwind' through which we steer our way. They may even see a consistent difference between 'higher' and 'lower' self, and identify the latter with a beast within, a body or a demon. I cannot see much moral reason why they should not. The muddled liberalism that denounces every effort to denounce or control the impulses of the human heart is no real rival to traditional psychology: all it does is relocate the enemy. So long as we are human, we shall inhabit a battlefield, and part of our long-term strategy will be to give a face and features to the enemies of our fragile order. Maybe our goal must be to 'lie down with the lions, like Daniel', as early scholiasts supposed the moral of Christ's stay in the wilderness, but we must not think that easy, or immediate, any more than we should pretend not to see experimental difficulties or theoretical contradictions in current science merely because we 'believe' that there will one day be a unified theory agreed by all parties.

But need we think of the relation between Beast and Angel as antagonistic? Must the only acceptable solution be angelic control over a fully chastened beast, obedient through fear and slavish affection? That has often been the image: everything, so Aristotle said, can be parsed as a composite of master and servant, form and matter, intellect and sensuality. If there is to be a single organism, the higher must control the lower, whereas 'wicked men' are at odds even with themselves (*Nicomachean Ethics* 8, 1159^b 7 ff.). And does this experience of tension or inner turmoil give any weight—as Plato thought it did (*Phaedo* 94 B 7 ff.)—to theories of a metaphysical distinction between 'soul' and 'body', or between 'intellect' and 'sensuality'?

Souls and Bodies

Before tackling that second question, I should remind you of my basic method: I am seeking to describe the human situation from within, phenomenologically, and not to offer a transcendental account of what gives rise to that experience. That something does give rise to it is my firm conviction: the social idealism or socio-solipsism that has engulfed some fashionable writers is not mine. I firmly believe that there is a reality essentially independent of all human cognition and experience which may none the less be known by us. I reject scepticism and idealism alike, for both amount to the same thing: 'adhering to appearances we live in accordance with the normal rules of life, undogmatically' (Sextus Empiricus 1933: 17 (1.23)). Those who purport to answer such sceptical puzzles as 'Descartes' Demon, or the Mad Neurologist' by suggesting that we cannot even pose or understand the question that is being asked, are themselves Sceptics in the ancient sense, people who have denied the importance of real truth. I do not share that view—partly because those who hold it, and who regularly sneer at the naïvety or presumed arrogance of realists like myself, seem to me to be involved in the most obvious of pragmatic self-contradictions. If I am *wrong* to be a realist, there is at least one 'fact of the matter' that is more than a social norm, and anti-realism is therefore false (and I am *not* wrong to be a realist). So if I am wrong, I am not wrong: therefore I am not wrong ('necessarily: if p implies not-p then not-p'). Some things are true whether we know them or not, and even whether we could ever know them or not. What 'we' really are is not necessarily quite obvious, and our experience does not contain the world. *Per contra*, there is a world contains us all, and on which we are founded. Our consciousness is not self-sustaining: it rests on something, no matter what, of which we are not conscious.

This is one meaning, at any rate, of Plato's insistence on the 'separateness' of Forms: 'true and just human behaviour cannot be based on the conventional concepts and standards to which public opinion clings' (Gadamer 1986: 18). Even if we come to the truth through educated sensibility that truth is more than what we now find 'obvious'.

But though I am a dogmatic and quite unembarrassed realist, I do believe that the proper way to explore the inner realms of our experience is from within, and that what sustains us, deeper than our self itself, can be appreciated as a sort of person—though that latter remark is, for the moment, by the way. Neurology, behavioural psychology, ethology are useful disciplines, but I have yet to see good reason to displace the ancient project on which they depend: namely, to identify and codify the realms of sensual and imaginative experience. Nothing that those 'objective' sciences show can reasonably convince me that I have no inner life. No aphorism that fashionable writers cite from Wittgenstein can do the job either. Inward exploration, irrespective of the underlying, and presently unknown reals that ground the possibility of such experience, is a real and honourable and rule-governed activity. Those who declare, bombastically, that 'folk-psychology' has not progressed since Sophocles (and thence infer the need to adopt a purely neurophysiological research programme), have plainly read little Sophocles, and no Plotinus, Augustine, Evagrius, or Teresa of Avila—let alone any Buddhist texts, or the meditation exercises of modern (Celt or Amerindian inspired) shamanism.

It is strange that thousands of men believe in atoms without having the slightest knowledge of the facts and calculations which confirm this hypothesis, while they decline to believe in their souls, of which at all events they know more than atoms. (Lutoslawski 1924: 149)

It is of that inner—which is not to say 'private'—world that D. H. Lawrence could sensibly say: 'it's no use telling me the Moon's a dead rock in the sky. I know it's not.' The merely material model of the universe, formed by deliberately excluding historical association or humane emotion, is not necessarily the only truth. At the very least, there are demonstrably some truths that cannot be incorporated in that model, and so must be investigated otherwise. It is better, I believe, not to adopt such methods as must beg the question against Lawrence or Lutoslawski. The final language, Peirce's ultimate consensus, may not be such as we, being what we are here-now, could comprehend. Maybe things as they are will turn out to be so different from all our categories that there will not even be any way of saying that 'we were wrong'. But that way lies madness: our only available practical epistemology must grant us the right to work from what we find, and not set arbitrary, methodological limits on what that must be.

So back to the soul, and its environment: the 'body' that Plato sometimes identified as the soul's enemy or tomb or insubordinate domestic, is not at first the body that physiologists inspect, or physicists conceive. It is the body of our experience, the body that each of us inhabits, lives, controls. I experience myself as being a body, a moving element of the material and social universe. The body I am (but also paradoxically am not) is one that hungers, thirsts, feels pleasurable aches from exercise. Its heart, my heart, pounds with fear or anger or excitement; its digestive system interferes with work; too many of its organs, which I live through, have their own drives and weaknesses. My lived body may even incorporate the tools or machines I use, the car I drive. If it does not, I am likely to drive quite badly, but even if it does, much more is going on in that machine than I can know. If we have very little influence even over the thoughts we entertain— as I have pointed out before—we have as little influence over most of those material processes we experience from within, and by which we do at first locate ourselves. It is as obvious as ever Plato wished that the life of our body does not develop or fall into any coherent order of its own: 'we' discipline that life, or fail to; we organize head, heart, and lungs, belly and limbs and gonads, and are often disconcerted by their excesses or defects.

The whirlwind of our thoughts and purposes, or the insufficiently cohesive Parliament of the Soul, as we live it, is not exhausted by those drives we label 'bodily'. First, that parliament makes some attempt to control and discipline the bodily drives, so demonstrating that there are other drives and purposes than those: some bodily organisms, no doubt, take shape and live without any distinct ruler or half-way centralized committee. Ours does not. Most animals, perhaps, experience no conflict in their lives: each motive and behaviour pattern has its place, and where there might be conflict some ritual or displacement activity has been invented by long ages of evolutionary change. Female spiders do not need to work out whether or not to eat prospective mates before or after mating. A reflective spider might have reason

to suppose herself a presence different from the bodily urges
she so exactly and appropriately feels. Consider fantasy a
moment, and James Tiptree's story, 'Love is the Game, the
Game is Death',[3] or Stapledon's plant-men. Fantasy aside,
there are other animals whose urges do not have an immanent
order: witness a young male chimpanzee diverted between a
bunch of bananas and a female chimp in heat (see Fromm
1974: 111 f.). Reflective chimpanzees would have reason to
distinguish themselves, their self-reflective, self-controlling
souls from their lived bodies. So do we, and find or create the
sort of soul we are by what we make our own. Warren,
summarizing Plotinus: 'the kind of man you are depends on
the center with which you identify yourself' (1964: 97).

But this phenomenological distinction between spirit and
flesh, the organizing hopes and reasons and the disruptive and
recalcitrant impulse, does not directly support any metaphysical distinction. Maybe both spirit and flesh are manifestations of one and the same reality, whether that is a physical
body or an unlocatable soul. That we have other interests and
reasons than the fleshly ones does not demonstrate that we are
not essentially physical things: metaphysical materialists do
not have to be 'materialists' in that other sense of 'sensualists'.
But at the same time it is also a fallacy to imagine that the
strength and unavoidability of our fleshly experience lends
any weight to metaphysical materialism. The bodies we
cannot escape, the insistent, 'necessary' drives of hunger,
thirst or lust, do not establish that we are 'really' physical
objects in an 'objective' (i.e. public, non-teleonomic, non-
affective) space-time. And Kant's puzzle, perhaps more than
Plato's, does have some resonance: the sensual happiness of
individuals could be better, more reliably achieved by
instinct, settled reaction-patterns, immanent order, than by
our reflective, ordering souls. What good does our intelligence
do us, or our line? Does it have any real evolutionary function,
or is it—at best—our one good example of an evolutionary
trend that has long since grown too monstrous for its victim's

---

[3] In which intelligent arachnoids seek to prevent themselves from
reverting to behaviour patterns that no longer match their personal
endeavours: how shall they stop themselves killing and eating their friends?

good?[4] Are these souls baroque monstrosities, or is their life, their object, something more than the effective ordering of fleshly drives? Are there other goals than those insistent appetites, and if there are, what world exists for their achievement?

The soul entombed in flesh, or barnacled with fleshly needs, or charitably supplied with instruments to handle its appointed task of managing this little segment of material reality (and all these descriptions are allowed by Plato) has its own goals, including that of understanding and admiring that which is. Could there be a 'pure soul', unencumbered by the flesh? Recent thinkers have denied the possibility, or claimed that at the least such souls could not be recognizable persons. They may be right, but we need, once again, to distinguish different oppositions. A pure soul in Plato's sense is one without fleshly appetites, and so no further need to organize those drives. Contemporary arguments against the mere possibility of a 'pure soul' are mostly concerned with the difficulty of reidentifying bodiless and essentially unlocatable beings: for such a being (supposing it to be) the thought that 'it was the same self as', for example, Sargon of Akkad could have no public confirmation or content. 'Being the same self as' could only amount to 'thinking oneself the same self as', since there would be no objective 'fact of the matter' to discern by any other route than the brute conviction of that self—but what then could such a conviction amount to? An attempted self-identification that could not be mistaken could not be correct either. 'Memory' of doing what Sargon of Akkad did, could not, even in principle, be distinguished from clairvoyant knowledge, and since no unseen apparatus is provided to support those 'memories' that are not currently on view such immediate clairvoyance, constantly repeated, seems a clearer bet.

These arguments are strong ones, though less decisive than some theologians suppose, but they are irrelevant to the

---

[4] Other proposed examples, as the antlers of the Great Elk (now extinct), are not undisputed. Those antlers were probably no larger, in proportion, than those of any other deer. But even if they were, we would have some story to explain their being so. What story do evolutionary theorists have to explain human intelligence that does not identify it as a great mistake?

Platonic case. Plato nowhere envisages a situation where others cannot recognize the unfleshed, pure soul: on the contrary, his Socrates looks forward, however impishly, to long conversations with the famous dead. The thrust of Plato's doctrine is that the pure Socrates will be 'even more a Socrates', stripped of everything that got in the soul's way. Such a Socrates might still have a snub-nose, and his 'real appearance', how he is for the eye of intellect, may accurately symbolize Socratic irony—as Plato causes Alcibiades to say (*Symposium* 215 A 17 ff.). Immortal beauty may be stripped of 'human flesh and colours and all the other mortal flummery' (*Symposium* 211 E 2 ff.), but that is to say it is not glimpsed through shadows, not that there is no way of identifying it as such. When Plotinus corrected Plato's expressed disdain for artists, he suggested that Pheidias had sculpted Zeus as Zeus would manifest to mortal sight (*Ennead* 1. 8. 1, 39–40). And Plato's account of the true earth's surface, in the *Phaedo*, similarly emphasizes that it is less muddy, less refracted than our ordinary vision allows. Plato, like Berkeley, expects

a happyness large as our desires, and those desires not stinted to ye few objects we at present receive from some dull inlets of perception, but proportionate to wt our faculties shall be wn God has given the finishing touches to our natures and made us fit inhabitants for heaven. (Berkeley 1948: vii. 12)

The present failings of our senses, and of our sensory bodies, are chiefly that they inadequately represent the realities that are struggling into being, or rather, on Platonic terms, already *are* but do not yet appear. Even the beast within is groping for immortal beauty.

How the Real Self Dreams Us Human

But can we, with that clue, begin to turn the story round? We experience ourselves as plural entities, negotiating bargains and repressing vagrant impulses in the name of some half-formulated notion of good order. There is, as the ancients knew, not one beast in the human heart, but many:

> Man is a lumpe, where all beasts kneaded be,
> Wisdome makes him an Arke where all agree.

(Donne 1929: 163)

What we chiefly symbolize as 'animal' are those lusts and fears that we can easily suppose to influence outward animals, or that outward animals most easily symbolize for us. The pride of the peacock and the lust of the goat and the wrath of the lion do not belong to those real creatures just as such, but to their images in human fancy, and we have Blake's word for it that they are respectively the glory, bounty, and the wisdom of God (Blake 1966: 151). 'The roaring of lions, the howling of wolves, the raging of the stormy sea, and the destructive sword, are portions of eternity, too great for the eye of man' (Blake 1966: 151).

What the ancients called an angel, a *daimon*, or a god is what we call a mood, a complex of images and compelling thoughts, a sudden rage of the spirit, that all of us may recognize as the 'same' thing manifested on many occasions of our own lives, and those of others. So the beasts within are just such *daimones*: demons, 'thieves and rebels', if they wrench us away from our good order, angels if they are 'servants to the infinite & Eternal of the Human form' (Blake 1966: 366, 571). And perhaps we may begin to allow that some of what we symbolize as beasts, excluded from the present order of our mundane personality, might carry messages from deeper down within. 'Once I dreamed that I was a butterfly, and then awoke to find I was a man. Now I do not know if I am a man who dreamed he was a butterfly, or a butterfly dreaming that he is Chuang Tzu.' Which is just the possibility that Jung was prepared to envisage:

My self retires into meditation and meditates my earthly form. To put it another way, it assumes human shape in order to enter three-dimensional existence, as if someone were putting on a diver's suit in order to dive into the sea.... This reversal [of the imagined relationship between ego-consciousness and the unconscious] suggests that in the opinion of the 'other side', our unconscious existence [i.e. the one of which 'we' here-now are unconscious] is the real one and our conscious world a kind of illusion, an apparent reality constructed for a specific purpose, like a dream which seems a reality as long as we are in it. (Jung 1967: 355 f.)

And if that real self dreams us 'human' how else should it appear in our present consciousness except as unhuman? 'When thou seest an Eagle, thou seest a portion of Genius; lift up thine head!' (Blake 1966: 152)

In brief: when some immortal element of the human condition manifests to us as an inner beast (or we see outer beasts as images of our own inner life), it may be demonic (as lacking an essential connection with, and obedience to, the real Form of Humanity), but it may also or alternatively be the only way that real Form itself could manifest to our distracted state. Duerr suggests (1985: 65) that the shaman 'becomes' an animal to be aware of his humanity. Rather than enlisting angels to repress the beast, we may occasionally ask ourselves if the beast is not an angel. Which aphorism should not be taken as equivalent to the consoling thought that after all we needn't discipline desires, any more than Blake intended to support indiscipline.

So perhaps current shamanistic exercise should be taken seriously. 'Current shamanism'? Professional philosophers should have no difficulty recognizing what I mean, since works of philosophy are regularly shelved next door to 'New Age' theses in bookshops and public libraries. On the other hand it is clearly important to most of us professionals to dissociate ourselves from merely occult or esoteric literature: how can one be taken seriously if one admits to reading stuff like that? I refuse to panic. Most such literature is repetitive and unconvincing—unconvincing especially if the author claims an insight that she must not convey to outsiders, or a special line to 'hidden masters' in the East, the West, or Outer Space, and especially if she shows no sign of seeing the grave perils that camp about the soul. 'Do-It-Yourself' shaman kits are a concession to an age that will not admit to ever being wrong, to needing correction, and that therefore prefers to think that 'the world is what we—personally—make it' rather than a reality to be explored in fear and trembling. True meditation is not an invitation to self-serving, pleasant fantasy, but the rigorous pursuit described—amongst many others—by Teresa of Avila (see Teresa 1961).

There are none the less some things to be learnt from contemporary efforts to understand and practice 'shamanism', whether the inspiration is drawn from Celtic or post-Celtic story (as Matthews 1985) or from Amerindian (as Harner 1982) or aboriginal ceremonial or from the romanticized nature-worship that has been equated—unhistorically—with European witchcraft. These traditions offer different maps of the soul, but do agree that a form of controlled imagination can put us in touch with powers deeper than the everyday, powers that reveal themselves to us in the shape of animals. If you set yourself to climb down an imagined hole, or through an imagined tunnel into the Underworld, you will find streams and trees, and also some 'totem-animal', 'familiar', 'spirit-friend'. Traditional identification of such forms with devils should not be dismissed too lightly: those who seek to summon godlings to the surface of our lives should remember that this was exactly what many earnest and hopeful Europeans were seeking to do in the years that led up to the triumph and fall of National Socialism. But if the gods are in service to the infinite and eternal of the human form they may be regarded as guardian angels, and reminders of the presence in us of something not ourselves.

5

Cognition, Revelation, and Inspiration

Vain Wisdom All and False Prophecy

Presently approved techniques of discovery require us to attend to those objects present to us through our senses, under whatever description contemporary science approves—though I have already observed that Galilean science owes far more to Platonism than to naïve empiricism. Ancient techniques required the initiate to turn around to examine what lay behind our ordinary self, to reverse customary expectations, to hang upside down above the well of Memory, as Odin did.

> As long as we continue to focus our attention outside ourselves we are like a creature with many faces surrounding a single brain, each face unaware of the others, and of his identity with them. Were one able to be spun around, either by his own effort or through the good fortune of being yanked by Athena herself, he will find himself face to face with the good, with himself, with the universe. (Lamberton 1986: 94, after Plotinus, *Ennead*, 6. 5. 7, 11–37)

The process of discovery was a spiritual one, in that it required a real moral effort, a change of heart, a spiritual circumcision, a flaying, a being-torn-to-pieces and buried alive: the old self, the ordinary citizen and human animal, was sacrificed to allow the single eye of shamanism to take shape in us.

> O the mind, mind has mountains; cliffs of fall
> frightful, sheer, no-man-fathomed. Hold them cheap
> may who ne'er hung there.
>
> (Hopkins 1970: 100)

Although it is still true—as I shall emphasize in a moment—that scholarship and science require a moral effort, and that the novice is being given a new soul, the public advantages of 'science' rest on the possibility that we may have the power without the moral cost. If a shaman or a yogi wishes to keep warm in winter, he must practice breath-control and mind-control until he can dry a sheet soaked in icy water by body-heat alone. When we wish to be warm, we simply turn on the heating, and forget the moral costs. The modern scientist—or the modern citizen who uses 'scientific discoveries' without understanding or moral effort—fulfils the ancient dream of the magician, to exercise power without having to reform the heart. Technology provides for all the powers that once were reserved—whether in reality or in fable—to those prepared to pay the price (which is, of course, not to want to use the powers). Fable also suggests that the kind of asceticism that thinks itself vindicated by the acquisition of such powers is not worth the price: witness the story of the ascetic who spent twenty years acquiring the merit to walk across a river which his brother could cross by paying the ferryman a penny (Weil 1987: 256; see also Duerr 1985: 105). But perhaps we should remember the aphorism Jung borrowed from an ancient: 'if the wrong man uses the right means, the right means work in the wrong way' (Jung 1967: 83). As Foster remarked (1967: 66):

It is noteworthy that what the scientific method attempts is to free other people from disabilities, without the precedent requirement of having freed oneself: i.e. to achieve the end [of building men and women who can resist the infection of warfever] by mastering a technique, i.e. to achieve it without repentance.

And remember Epictetus's devasting rebuke to a would-be philosophy lecturer:

The affair is momentous, it is full of mystery, not a chance gift, nor given to all comers . . . You are opening up a doctor's office although you possess no equipment other than drugs, but when or how these drugs are applied you neither know nor have ever taken the trouble to learn . . . Why do you play at hazard in matters of the utmost moment? If you find the principles of philosophy entertaining sit down and turn them over in your mind all by yourself, but don't ever call yourself a philosopher. (*Discourses* 3. 21. 17)

What matters in philosophy—anciently so called—is not the abstract solution of theoretical puzzles—as we now understand

the term 'theoretical'—but the sort of truth that can inform
the heart. *Noein,* as Heidegger pointed out (1968: 203), does
not mean 'to think' as we now mean 'thinking', but 'to take to
heart'.

The dissociation of moral and intellectual concerns characteristic of
our own way of thinking—lead[s] us to consider it absurd and
impertinent to inquire closely into the degree of moral virtue
possessed by a candidate for a Chair of Philosophy and to require
him, if he was even to be put on the short list, to be free from envy
and ambition and indifferent to such worldly considerations as the
salary scale. (Armstrong 1970: 228)

In another sense, of course, technology and its associated
sciences are not magical. Magic, in that other sense, is the
belief that 'wishing makes it so', that we can change the world
by talking differently about it. Existentialists and social
relativists are the would-be magicians of our day, refusing to
admit the existence of a real world independent of 'our'
wishes. Some of these continue to speak as if there is at least a
world of 'morally neutral' fact to which we can be true, as
though it were easier to tell any moral story that we liked than
any 'neutral' or 'factual' one. I have observed before that
those who abandon 'moral realism' must usually end up
abandoning 'scientific realism' as well. At the very least, we
have as good historical evidence for the ineluctability of moral
truism, as for the 'hardness' of scientific theory. In those days,
Thucydides said of the early years of the Peloponnesian War,
'words changed their ordinary meanings and were construed
in new senses. Reckless daring passed for the courage of a
loyal partisan, far-sighted hesitation was the excuse of a
coward, moderation was the pretext of the unmanly, the
power to see all sides of a question was complete inability to
act' (*History of the Peloponnesian War* 3. 82). So it was that
Athens gradually dissipated all her moral capital.

As it will be in the future, it was at the birth of man—
there are only four things certain since social progress began:
that the dog returns to his vomit and the sow returns to her mire,
and the burnt fool's bandaged finger goes wabbling back to the fire;
and that after this is accomplished and the brave new world begins
when all men are paid for existing and no man must pay for his sins,

as surely as water will wet us, as surely as fire will burn,
the Gods of the Copybook Headings with terror and slaughter
return!

(Kipling 1927: 718 f.)

Kipling's conviction, and my own suspicion, is that those
'copybook headings' are records of the real experience of
humankind, and that they constitute 'moral facts' as ineluctable as any 'morally neutral' ones. Courage, temperance,
fidelity, civility, prudence are Aristotelian virtues over all the
world, whatever we choose to call them, and whether we
notice them or not. There is more agreement over all the
world about such virtues than about any matter of 'mere fact',
and a proper submission to the leadings of nature as we seek
to come to terms with facts instead of fancies will constantly
remind us of them. If we teach our children to admire greed
and rebellious conceit, we can hardly complain if the civil
peace is broken (see Weil 1987: 223 f.). If we proclaim that
fornication and adultery are harmless fun, and that the
prohibition of incest is outmoded superstition, why should we
be surprised if sexual 'abuse' of children grows?

I do not mean only that there is an analogy between
discovering, say, the correct laws of Newtonian mechanics
and remembering (for we hardly need to discover) simple
moral truisms. There is, simply in that both may require us to
put aside our wishes and received opinions. But there is more
than an analogy here: the practice of scientific enquiry itself is
a moral and obedient one. Introductory works on scientific
method hardly seem to realize this, and limit their few
paragraphs on 'scientific ethics' to warnings not to steal
another scientist's results, or falsify one's own. Even the Royal
College of Veterinary Surgeons produce a handbook on ethics
which is far more concerned with the size and position of the
veterinarian's plate than with spelling out the implications of
veterinary concern for animal welfare. At a verbal level such
works promote the other image of scientific enquiry, which I
mentioned at the start of this chapter: the morally neutral one,
equally at the service of virtue and of vice. 'Scientists', *qua*
scientists, are not to have any moral views, which are to be
counted as merely subjective commitments, over and above
the 'professional ethics' of a particular guild. This does not

usually seem to stop scientists from claiming the prestige due to their guild for the particular moral views they choose on occasion to proclaim, at the same time as they profoundly resent any rational examination of them by 'outsiders'. Modernists in general, as Sandel points out, are rarely restrained by their professed agnosticism about the Big Questions from taking the 'Meaningless Void' for granted as the necessary condition for the 'self-directing individuals' busily 'creating their own meanings' (Sandel 1982: 176) to whom they smugly appeal.

But the rhetoric of moral neutrality is at once a betrayal of civil and human duty and also quite inadequate to the very enterprise on which such scientists are engaged. The scientific, and more generally the scholarly, enterprise is essentially a moral one, the pursuit of valuable truth by those who think themselves obliged to give up personal fears or wishes and to order their lives accordingly. Once that is recognized as a moral commitment it can be rationally criticized: we can sensibly ask whether 'the truth' should be pursued no matter what the necessary method was, or what likely consequences of discovery or publicity, or neglect of other duties might ensue. The occasional demand for absolute freedom of scientific enquiry from all other duties, or for the claim of individual researchers to follow their 'own' conscience (especially when that turns out to be the internalized prejudice of their particular clan or sect), amounts to that 'right of clergy' to be tried only by church courts or their own conscience that no civil society could possibly allow. To suppose that mere curiosity, unsupported by moral arguments, has special rights to satisfaction (as if 'I want to know what broiled baby tastes like, or why it tastes like that' were a better excuse for cannibalism than 'I want to enjoy the taste'), is just silly; to suppose that there is a particular moral duty to find out and publicize 'the truth' only makes sense within a seriously intended moral system that will also acknowledge other values. Maybe there is, after all, one truth that is worth everything to know, but it is unlikely to be a truth that modern scientists or scholars are going to reveal. I remind you again of Blish's fantasy of Armageddon, where the black magician explains himself to a more conventional scientist as wicked as himself: ' "I think what I'm after is worth the risk [of damnation], and what I'm after is something you understand perfectly, and for which you've sold your own soul, or if you prefer a slightly less loaded word, your integrity, to [a war-mongering arms-dealer]—knowledge" ' (1967: 78).[1] Blish's fable is, consciously, absurd at many levels, not least in the magician's expressed conviction that it will be worth being eternally damned to have found out about (and then in hell either to have forgotten or to have had turned to agonized remembrance) some necessarily finite segment of God's creation—which the redeemed, in any case, will have eternity to know and to enjoy. The magician indeed recognizes his own absurdity before the end: what was his desire for unlimited knowledge but an instance of gluttony, doomed to be disappointed? 'More! More! is the cry of a mistaken soul; less than All cannot satisfy Man' (Blake 1966: 97). But though the fable is rationally absurd, it precisely expresses the devotion to some one aspect of the Infinite and Eternal of the Human Form (whether it be curiosity or lust or anger or security) that renders that a thief and rebel.

> From this disease of curiosity it is that some dive towards the discovery of secrets in Nature, whereof the knowledge—though not beyond our ken—doth profit nothing, yet men desire to know it for the sake of knowing. From this perverse desire of knowledge also it groweth that men inquire into things by magical arts. (Augustine, *Confessions* 10. 35: 1923: 311).

Curiosity, as I remarked in an earlier chapter, can be as great a source of evil as greed or outraged pride:

> To St Bernard, whose *Nosce Te ipsum* describes the spiritual discipline of self-knowledge, the primary step off the path in the wrong direction was not pride, not sloth, not lust—but curiositas. St Bernard speaks mainly of its destructiveness in regard to oneself, of the harm the curious mind can have upon peace of soul and spiritual enlightenment. The ego, with its light, attempts to ferret out causes in hidden recesses of the personality, searches for detailed childhood memories, promises sweet sessions of silent introspection. We are

---

[1] Those who suppose that only deliberate cruelty, if that, is damnable, should be reminded that our Lord thought otherwise: it is indifference that he decries.

curious to know who we are and how we got this way, whereas the religious attitude would recognize from the first that we are God's creatures and we are what we are owing to His purpose working in the soul rather than to accidents of upbringing and circumstance. (Hillman 1967: 18 f.)

Hillman himself speaks of the harm morbid or perverted curiosity, 'sublimated scoptophilia or voyeurism, the lubricity of vicarious living through another's dirt and thrills', does to those others. There are things, even about ourselves, that it is better not to know.

> I cast for comfort I can no more get
> by groping round my comfortless, than blind
> eyes in their dark can day or thirst can find
> thirst's all-in-all in all a world of wet.
> Soul, self; come, poor Jackself, I do advise
> you, jaded, let be; call off thoughts awhile
> elsewhere; leave comfort root-room; let joy size
> at God knows when to God knows what.
>
> (Hopkins 1970: 103)

So what form of Knowledge could it be that should serve—as others than deracinated intellectuals have expected—as the essence of human or more than human well-being? Augustine himself insisted that 'to joy in the truth is the desire of all men', and applauded that desire (*Confessions* 10. 23: 1923: 293). What sort of moral discipline could *sapientia* require (see Weil 1987: 226 f.)? What must we suppose the structure of a soul capable of this (or any other) knowledge? What must the world be to allow us knowledge? What might the relation be between magic and philosophy, in any of the senses of those shifty terms?

Truth and the Inner Light

I have already insisted, upon many occasions, that the only sort of world in which anyone could reasonably expect to find out real truths is a world created and sustained by God. 'Knowledge of the world is possible because God has patterned the world after the divine ideas. Man can know the world because God has given man an awareness of the eternal forms by which he can judge sensations and form *scientia*' (Nash 1969: 123)—as Nash summarizes St Augustine. In God's absence some form of pragmatic anti-realism seems inevitable. If we are to be realists, we had better be theists too. That does not constitute, nor was it offered as, a 'proof' of 'God's existence'. It is a reminder of the context within which Truth and Knowledge used to be values, and a suggestion that in a supposedly godless universe knowledge as such is neither absolutely valuable nor likely to be possible. Believing in God, amongst other things, just is believing that there is a discoverable truth that it must be our chief endeavour to find out and make our own. That discoverable truth may not be, probably is not, all the truth there is. A further aspect of a properly humble and theistic realism is an awareness that there are truths forever beyond our reach, that Caesar had porridge for breakfast on his seventh birthday or that he didn't, that Fermat's Last Theorem is true and provable, or that it's not, that the First Unfallen Kingdom and other such imagined 'possible worlds' are 'really real', but occupy some radically 'other' space or angelic *aevum* (see Devlin in Hopkins 1959*a*: 112) accessible only through God's special providence, or that they're not. There are, the realist supposes, all sorts of truths that we do not, cannot, or need not ever know. All our knowledge rests within an unbounded sea of ignorance. As Augustine pointed out (*Confessions* 10. 5), I do not even know all about 'my very own' mind and memory. My self, so far from being Cartesian and transparent, is Augustinian, Plotinian, and opaque.

'The true definition of science is this: the study of the beauty of the world' (Weil 1987: 250). What we can come to know is what God has set in us to know. Plato's question stands (as Augustine also recognized): how can we recognize anything as being *true* if we do not know what truth is?

For that woman in the Gospel had lost her groat and sought it with a light, and unless she had remembered it, she had never found it. For after it was found, how could she have known whether it was the same or not, unless she had remembered it? (*Confessions* 10. 8: 1923: 286)

Every attempted methodology rests on some presumed account of what has the very taste and form of truth, whether it be 'clearness and distinctness of ideas', or immediate sensibility, or merely that complacent egoism which some name 'a robust sense of reality'. You may remember Screwtape's client (Lewis 1955: 13), whom 'a healthy dose of "real life" (by which he meant the bus and the newsboy) was enough to show that "all that sort of thing" just couldn't be true'. On any reasonable view it is only if we have already encountered truth in our inward parts that anything else can be recognized as true.

Augustine said, 'Accordingly, even though I speak about true things, I still do not teach him who beholds the true things, for he is taught not through my words but by means of the things themselves which God reveals within the soul'. (Nash 1969: 90, after *De Magistro* 12)

So what is this truth that I must already possess, even if under the guise of forgetfulness ('nor can we be said to have entirely forgotten that which we remember ourselves to have forgotten, for that lost notion which we have entirely forgotten we cannot so much as seek for' (*Confessions* 10. 19: 1923: 288)), if I am to recognize anything as being wholly or partly or probably or possibly true?

Behold in those fields and caves and innumerable dens of my Memory, innumerably full of innumerable kinds of things, whether they be brought in by images, as all bodies are, or by the presence of the things themselves, as the arts are, or by I know not what notions or impressions as the affections of the mind, which the memory holds even when the mind feeleth them not, since whatsoever is in the mind is also in the memory, behold, I say, how through all these I run about and flutter on this side and that, and I penetrate into them as deeply as I can, but without finding of any bottom. (10. 17: 1923: 285)

That God which is the Truth, which is not the mind, but the Lord and God of the mind (10. 25: 1923: 295), has yet a lodging in our memory, 'and there do I find thee when I call thee to remembrance and take delight in thee' (10. 24).

In every place, O Truth, thou givest audience to such as consult thee, and at the same time dost thou answer all their demands, be they never so diverse. Thou givest them clear answers, but everyone doth not clearly understand thee. For all men consult thee about what they will, but they do not always hear what they will by way of answer. He is thy best servant who endeavoureth not to hear that from thee which he desireth but rather desireth that which he heareth from thee. (10. 26: 1923: 296)

The Horizon of Knowledge

That all forms of knowledge are good, that 'to know' is God, is as inadequate and dangerous a claim as the pleasant equation of love and God.

To presume that every experience of love is Love of the Divine Ground of Being, to imagine that deep personal meaningfulness surmounts the pitch and hurdles of love's intricacies and can be the criterion for justification of unsanctified love, to be cozened into love by a philosophy which neglects its fearfulness (for if God is love then the beginning of wisdom is the fear of love), and to call this naïve ignorance of the shadow side of loving 'Honest to God' is witness to just how much of love lies in shadow . . . A psychologist must ask his clerical colleagues: why are you prey to these sophistries, these simple solutions; why do you blur the hierarchies of transcendence and ultimacy, neglecting the worlds of difference, represented traditionally by planes of being and classes of angels, between the levels and kinds of love . . . how can you equate falling-in-love with coming home to the Godhead? (Hillman 1967: 74 f.)

Even Aphrodite is a terrible divinity, and rightly feared: how much more that 'Love that moves the sun and other stars'? It is an easy thing to see signs of 'love' in the storm that destroys our enemy's house, as Blake remarked. Less easy when we are ourselves 'the prey of the gales':

They fought with God's cold—
and they could not and fell to the deck
(crushed them) or water (and drowned them) or rolled
with the sea-romp over the wreck.
Night roared, with the heart-break hearing a heart-broke rabble,
the woman's wailing, the crying of child without check—
till a lioness arose breasting the babble,
a prophetess towered in the tumult, a virginal tongue told.

(Hopkins 1970: 57)

What Hopkins's nun saw, so Hopkins tells, was

> the Master,
> ipse, the only one, Christ, King, Head:
> he was to cure the extremity where he had cast her.

Her experience, as Hopkins 'selved' it, was of the 'Ground of being, and granite of it', that he addressed in the opening of the poem (turned down by *The Month* in 1875 as 'metrically odd'):

> Thou mastering me
> God! giver of breath and bread;
> world's strand, sway of the sea;
> Lord of living and dead;
> Thou hast bound bones and veins in me, fastened me flesh,
> and after it almost unmade, what with dread,
> thy doing; and dost thou touch me afresh?
> Over again, I feel thy finger and find thee.

As Duns Scotus declared: 'to know any being as "this being" is already to conceive God in a very indistinct way; for "being" is included as part of the concept' (1962: 18). Sebastian Moore, in one of the few philosophically illuminating articles on Hopkins, summarizes his Scotist point as follows: 'the experience here is a complex of two inseparable components: the bringing himself to a point, walling himself in—in—to uniqueness; and the felt relation to God' (1944: 186). It is in recognizing something, and oneself, as unique, in being most present to oneself, that one is aware of one's relation to God.

Neither do I deny that God is so deeply present to everything that it would be impossible for him but for his infinity not to be identified with them, or from the other side, impossible but for his infinity so to be present to them. This is oddly expressed, I see; I mean, a being so intimately present as God is to other things would be identified with them were it not for God's infinity or were it not for God's infinity he would not be so intimately present to things. (Hopkins 1959a: 128: see Cotter 1972: 128)

The experience of presence which Hopkins records and evokes, has echoes in other writers, notably Stapledon: witness the Patagonian Boy's experience of being lost in a snow-drift, and suddenly seeing '[him]self and all of us through the eyes of the umpire' (1963: 110). Being Stapledon, he represents that umpire's gaze as 'exultant, almost derisive, yet not unkindly', where Hopkins saw instead.

> the Christ of the Father compassionate, fetched in the storm
> of his strides . . .
> the heaven-flung, heart-fleshed, maiden-furled
> miracle-in-Mary-of-flame,
> mid-numberèd he in three of the thunder-throne!

The style and the moral differ: Hopkins himself recognized, more staunchly perhaps than Stapledon, that 'there is an infinity of possible strains of action and choice for each possible self in [the infinity of possible] worlds and the sum of these strains would be also like a pomegranate in the round, which God sees whole but of which we see at best only one cleave [or exposed face]. Rather we see the world as one cleave and the life of each person as one vein or strain of colour in it' (1959*a*: 151).

Or as Cotter summarizes:

God sees the whole from within: he is the pleroma, pomegranate, or burl of all being. The cleave cut on the outside surface is what man sees, this universe, himself: the one opening of his thought and being inscaping sharply to the centre within—Christ. The world then is open, a source from which stress springs and a stem through which man's instress flows back to the king and through which man's instress flows back to the king and head. Through this infinitesimal fissure man glimpses and possesses the infinite I AM. (Cotter 1972: 44)

There is an ontological point already visible in this account of Hopkins, a way of considering the Incarnation that I hinted at—without realizing that it was to be found in Hopkins (as Hopkins 1959*a*: 170, 196 ff.; see Cotter 1972: 124 ff.)—in my paper in Macquarrie's *Festschrift*: 'in this way Christ is the firstborn among creatures'. But that is a theme for my next volume. I have devoted some time to Hopkins's evocation of the experience of Presence, of inscape, unique identity, and of the relation of any created thing to its infinite Ground, by way of reminding us all that philosophical argument and thought must not be abstract. 'The affair is momentous, not a chance gift nor given to all comers'. But the matter which I have now described poetically and evocatively can be described more dryly. Hopkins did not begin from Scotus, nor even—quite— from personal experience. As Bender pointed out, his first use of the term 'inscape' was in some notes on Parmenides, whom modern philosophers do not generally approach enthusi- astically even if they honour him as an abstract theoretician prepared to follow the argument into any number of unlikely places.

Parmenides' great text, which he repeats with religious conviction, is that Being is and Not-being is not—which perhaps one can say, a little over-defining his meaning, means that all things are upheld by instress and are meaningless without it. . . . His feeling for instress, for the flush and foredrawn, and for inscape is most striking and from this one can understand Plato's reverence for him as the greater father of Realism. (Hopkins 1959*b*: 127)

It is perhaps a little difficult to decide whether to explain Parmenides through Hopkins or Hopkins through Parmenides! But the hint is a helpful one. Whereas Cartesians have supposed that the most certain proposition must be that I Exist, and left the indelible impression that this I is just the ordinary ego, and that solipsism is the only really rational imagining, Parmenides, back at the beginning of analytical philosophy, knew better. The axiom of the Way of Truth is that IT IS, and it is not possible for IT NOT TO BE. That I exist, i.e. that there is a single and enduring subject of experience distinct from those experiences, or that such a subject could be identified with what it seems to know about itself, or that it could be conceived or exist even if there were no publicly ascertainable realities, are all profoundly uncertain dicta. Parmenides saw that Truth existed, that there was One Truth. If the demon or the mad neurologist creates an illusion even of Cartesian identity, and deceives no one since there is none to be deceived, yet it will still be true that something then is true—namely the story I have just told. The one incontrovertible and absolute beginning of all science is just this: the True exists. By this I mean, not that there are true propositions but that there is That by reference to which such propositions are 'true'.

Not only does it exist: there is only one of It. It cannot even be thought that there are two Truths, two Realities. 'It is one, only-begotten, motionless, eternal. How could Being perish? How could it come into Being? If it came into being, it is not; and so too if it is about-to-be at some future time. Thus Coming-into-being is quenched, and Destruction also into the unseen.' 'For Hopkins, the insights of Parmenides are not merely conceptual, but involve acts of faith in Being that "heeds but hides, bodes but abides" ' (1970: 62). Man gives a real assent, his "yes", to "is" ' (Cotter 1972: 16). That is also, recognizably, the thought since associated with Heidegger.

IT IS, and I AM, are both names of the One Reality we cannot think away. We encounter It 'in the act of knowing [ourselves] asserting existence, not in the abstract, but in the concrete world of objects that [we] know. This intuitive judgemental contact with Being as the coalescing plenum of the universe is inscape, the IS of all things that are, which leads back directly in turn to instress, the foredrawing or ingathering ·act of recognition: the giving back of being to Being' (Cotter 1972: 14). Or as Jonathan Edwards—quoted on an earlier occasion— put it: 'the cordial consent of beings to Being in general'— which is not 'being-in-the-abstract', but the one concrete reality. In the act of knowing ourselves asserting existence we know ourselves under judgement, the undying light of Heracleitos.

TRUTH is what cannot be thought away, and which looms in our experience of the unique identity of every partial thing. IS is guaranteed by the very thought of IT, and would be even if IT were never thought of. That Truth is single, because it cannot be that there *are* two truths: if there were *that* would itself be the one truth. IT is unchanging: for were it not, there would first be one truth and then another, and that very truth would itself not change. To prefer what is not true—though Parmenides would rightly say that there is no thing that is not an undivided part of Truth—is to live enclosed in what should only have been—and only is, in the light of eternity—a single element of truth, to choose one cleave out of the burl of being, the sum of all possible worlds held, as possibilities, within the single truth. That option, terribly enough, is real. 'This throwing back or confinement of [the rebel angels'] energy is a dreadful constraint or imprisonment' (Hopkins 1959*a*: 137).

> Where lies your landmark, seamark, or soul's star?
> There's none but truth can stead you. Christ is truth . . .
> Man lives that list, that leaning in the will
> no wisdom can forecast by gauge or guess,
> the selfless self of self, most strange, most still,
> fast furled and all foredrawn to No or Yes.
>
> (Hopkins 1970: 196 f.)

Saying 'No' is possible, and the result is also delineated by the poet's art:

> I am gall, I am heartburn. God's most deep decree
> bitter would have me taste: my taste was me;
> bones built in me, flesh filled, blood brimmed the curse.
> Selfyeast of spirit a dull dough sours. I see
> the lost are like this, and their scourge to be
> as I am mine, their sweating selves; but worse.
>
> (Hopkins 1970: 101; see 1959*a*: 262)

Or as Heracleitos said it: 'for those who've woken up there is one common world; each sleeper's turned aside to a private one' (22 B 89 DK).

There is a danger in the thesis that in IT we have an object guaranteed by the very thought of IT: Iris Murdoch's atheistical priest McAllister (1987: 488 ff.) identifies the soul's longing for God with God, but that is to place too much trust and love-liking in one's own fancy. 'Selfyeast of spirit a dull dough sours', and 'subjectivity' is *not, pace* Cupitt, 'the only divinity'. *Per contra*, 'religion's passionate interest is in a truth which is not merely something posited by its own passion and actual only in that passion, but in a truth which is independent of it and prior to it' (Cupitt 1971: 43). Were the sleeper to lose all link with IT there would be no sleeper left at all, nor any soured dough. Even dejection, damnation, and despair leave crannies open to 'the lights lit at the festival of the "peaceful Trinity" ' (Hopkins 1959*a*: 197). That common world, the Being in which we share, is present to any one of us, in our immediate sense, as the first deliverance of reason properly so called. One extract from the Rig-Veda, known to Hopkins:

Self is the Lord of all things, Self is the King of all things. As all the spokes of a wheel are contained in the nave and the circumference, all things are contained in this Self; all selves are contained in this self. Brahman itself is but Self. (Cotter 1972: 17)

That is the knowledge that is worth having, that is worth bringing forward to our conscious attention. The Self it names is not this ego, nor this animal organism here, although it is made evident exactly in the occasional self-awareness of this creature here, and of other things here in the world. Or as Solovyev put it, from a different angle: 'every one of us, every human being, is essentially and actually rooted, and takes part in, the universal or absolute man' (Solovyev 1948: 163). 'Every individual separateness is only a passing dream' (1948: 165). To recapitulate: knowledge is only possible, and only obligatory, if we have already got the Truth, our Master, deep within our selves. Hopkins expresses this, maybe correctly, as the presence of Christ. Christ is to be our landmark, seamark, the goal, *skopos*, of our endeavour. Only an identity focused on the revelation in us of the One Truth is rooted in the eternal, and that One Truth is in us as Jesus, the very form of humanity. But the doctrine is not simply a piece of Christian apologetic. A very ancient vocabulary and doctrine is applied to the Galilean *hasid* executed under Pontius Pilate, but that doctrine and vocabulary is intelligible without such historical reference. One of the oddest features of modern nominally Christian theology is the extent to which it is recognized that patristic theology relies upon an older systematic philosophy, and thence inferred that the 'Christian message' must be disentangled from that system merely because it strikes moderns as obscure. What is left of the message once we have forgotten philosophy is still more obscure.

[In certain books of the Platonists] I read, not indeed the express words, but the same thing in substance, and supported by many reasons of several kinds, that in the beginning was the Word and the Word was with God . . . Further, that the soul of man, though it gave testimony to the light is not yet the light; but the Word, God himself, is the true light . . . but I read not that the Word was made flesh and dwelt among us. (Augustine, *Confessions* 7. 9: 1923: 178)

Augustine's judgement was substantially correct. That the

One Truth, which lies even beyond being (when 'being' is understood to mean finite existence), is present to human intellect as the intellectual light, as *nous*, or Zeus, was common doctrine.[2] Only because that light rested in us could we hope to have any knowledge of anything at all; because it did we might be able to turn around to contemplate the divine intellect, and the One. We grasp the One only through the *Logos*. '*Nous*', I should add, here stands for that 'active or poietic *nous*' that Aristotle distinguished from the mere capacity of our animal organisms to intuit reasons. Whatever Aristotle intended to convey, many of his successors thought that there could be only one such discarnate, active *nous*, and that it was identical with the Divine *Logos*, itself the only-begotten of the Father. Myself, I think it very likely that Aristotle did mean that, but even if he did not, the doctrine was historically influential. Vycinas (1972: 63) offers a similar interpretation of Egyptian mythological thought: 'the ultimate reality, Atum . . . always remained beyond the horizons. By breaking into the openness of the horizons Atum becomes Ra. Nature, Atum, comes to light or disclosure through Ra, the god of the life-giving sun'. It is difficult, even impossible, to assess this as a genuine historical comment on the life-world of the Egyptians, but it is—or so I suspect—enormously closer to the truth of their experience and belief than merely materialistic assessments of their factual errors or patronizing comments on their heathen adoration of half-men and beasts (such as, I should add, both Augustine and Hopkins made).

What Vycinas is getting at is the ancient recognition that the One becomes present to us just in our engagement in a world, inevitably and rightly a human world, that structures our further responses. 'This reality which the sun mimics where will it rise from? What horizon will it lift itself over to make its appearance?' (*Ennead* 5. 5. 8, 3–8). That world becomes present to us when we feel, hear, glimpse 'behind' us the presence of the One. The human world opened before us may be only one cleave from the infinite 'pomegranate', and

---

[2] Though Plotinus usually preferred to allegorize Greek myth by punningly identifying Cronos as the divine *nous*, containing all divinities within himself (*Ennead* 5. 1. 7, 27 ff.). Zeus is rather the Life (*to zen*) that proceeds from the One and the Intellect together.

'of human nature the whole pomegranate fell in Adam' (Hopkins 1959a: 171), so that we are dogged by delusion and self-enclosed despair. Faith here is the lived conviction that there is a way back into the centre, and an absolute necessity if we are not to vanish into fantasy.

> We guess; we clothe Thee, unseen King,
> with attributes we deem are meet;
> each in his own imagining
> sets up a shadow in Thy seat.
>
> (Hopkins 1970: 33)

By this account, please note, there can be little real distinction between cognition and revelation. All genuine knowledge is of the form of revelation and response, a relationship with the one source of being. Ramanujan, 'self-taught mathematician', declared that his discoveries were dictated to him by a goddess. What else could do so? It does not follow that just any bright idea is the word of God, that all claims to contain the world's design are right. On the contrary, a proper cognitive obedience submits to correction. Scotus cites Augustine (*De Trinitate* 9. 6) with approval:

'Just because [infidel philosophers] argue most truly that all that happens in time takes place on account of eternal reasons, are they therefore able to perceive therein how many kinds of animals exist or how many seeds of each there were in the beginning and so on . . . Have they not sought all these things not by that unchangeable knowledge, but by the history of places and times, and have they not believed the written experience of others?' He means that contingent truths known by the senses alone or believed on the account of others are not known through the eternal rules. And yet special illumination is required even more for what must be believed than for necessary truths. (Duns Scotus 1962: 127)

Those who imagine that they already have a map to all the illimitable caverns and countries of the created universe are claiming a revelation greater than most God-fearers dare. The fact of Being, and its ultimate intelligibility, are both 'revealed', 'disclosed' to anyone who exercises a proper intellectual humility. The presence of Truth in us also makes it likely that the forms, the map or blueprint of the world, may also surface in our reflection. But such shapes and fantasies as we ordinarily and naturally intuit cannot, to say the least, be certainly equated with the *Logos*. In the Unfallen Kingdom, we may suppose, rational creatures were always guided right, but our condition is a fallen one. And in any case, even the unfallen Adam, being composite of sense and intellect, presumably had some use for sense: Adam could be surprised by things not mentioned or not detailed on his map. Angelic intellects, perhaps, could instantly intuit all the world's ways—though tradition tells us that such intellects themselves have unanswered questions! 'Reality is what method does not allow us to foresee' (Weil 1978: 73).

There is a great deal of anecdotal evidence about the origins of innovative theory that is at any rate compatible with the system that I am sketching. New theories do not come by strict deduction from old evidence. Often enough, the investigator's efforts must be to find the evidence for a theory that she already knows or suspects is true—which in no way contradicts the equal requirement of critical scholarship and experiment. 'When you have satisfied yourself that the theorem is true, you start proving it' (Polya 1954: 76).

> Watch narrowly
> the demonstration of a truth, its birth,
> and you trace back the effluence to its spring
> and source within us; where broods radiance vast,
> to be elicited ray by ray, as chance
> shall favour.
>
> (R. Browning, *Paracelsus* 1)

Galileo, asked why he was sure that different weights still fell at the same speed, replied that he was 'first convinced by reason rather than made certain by sense' (see Shea 1972: 157), adding by the way, that 'astronomers would never achieve any progress if they abandoned their system every time they encountered an apparently refractory phenomenon' (Shea 1972: 148). Science and all scholarship, in short, rests upon the faith that there is a key, that we do not now possess it, but that we can receive hints and teasing suggestions, often represented to us in symbolic guises, if only we put ourselves in the right frame of mind. This is exactly the technique that one might expect to work if the sciences were what Bacon scathingly insisted they were not: namely, the work of 'spirits and genii'! We therefore have as good evidence as we could reasonably expect that the world itself is founded on an intellectual Form, the *Logos*, known to us—except by special revelation—only in the scattered and sometimes misleading shape of a diverse assembly of principles.

When a man writes any work of genius or invents some creative action, is it now because some knowledge or power has come into his mind from beyond his mind? (Yeats 1955: 272)

Our history speaks of opinions and discoveries, but in ancient times when, as I think, men had their eyes ever upon those doors [of larger minds than the ordinary], history spoke of commandments and revelations. (Yeats 1961: 44)

Which has two final morals: first, that the scientific and scholarly enterprise is itself a moral and religious one, even if ill-formulated and opaque. Second, that the religious enterprise, so to call what is in this our fallen world a vastly diffuse and often hellish activity, should itself be seen in more rigorously cognitive terms. Panic fear of those who claim to 'know' God's will for all of us, and mild contempt for their failed prophecies, are understandable reactions, but it does not follow from those sins and errors that a merely sentimental agnosticism will serve us better. I have also often had occasion to notice that those who strongly disapprove of what they call 'fundamentalist religion' themselves display a quite extraordinary dogmatism about the world, their fellow-citizens, and their own purity of motive. Socrates' claim to ignorance was clearly ironic: too many of us—and of course I include myself in the charge—are tolerant only of what we do not mind about, and open-minded about everything but the truth of our convictions. If truth cannot be discovered in the religious realm, it cannot be discovered anywhere, for as Spengler remarked, 'there is no natural science without a precedent religion' (1926: ii. 380). 'What peculiar privilege has this little agitation of the brain which we call "thought", that we must thus make it the model of the whole universe?' (Hume 1976: 168) What indeed? But Hume's question marks the death of science as well as of theology, and if we refuse to let either perish, we must at last admit that 'thought' is not an 'agitation of the brain', but our way back into the Infinite.

6

Death and the Making of the Individual

The Practice of Death

The Philosophy which Epictetus thought momentous was otherwise known as the practice of death. Just so, 'the !Kung healer is the one who has looked death in the eye' (Duerr 1985: 68). It is a thought that commentators sometimes sentimentalize by the suggestion that 'their own death' is not a thing that reasonable people worry much about. Death, we are solemnly informed, is not an event in life, and everyone is immortal as long as she is alive (see Hearne 1986: 163 f. after Wittgenstein 1961: 6.4311)—and presumably insomniac as long as she is awake (see Clark 1983: 168)! If death is the end, we shall not notice that we are dead. 'It is an easy thing to triumph in the summer sun' (Blake 1966: 290), and easy to say, in the careful abstract, that only the misguided want to live for ever, that death comes like a sleep or like a culmination, since all finite being must at last exhaust its possibilities. The children's riddle defines our state:

> This thing all things devours,
> birds, beasts, trees and flowers.
> Slays king, ruins town,
> and beats high mountain down.

The approved answer, you may recall, is 'Time', but that is just to say that time, for us, is death. Which is why the Tarot's figure of Death carries a scythe and an hourglass. Taking one's troubles philosophically, in ordinary speech, is still to take them as a good Stoic might, as an inevitable aspect of our being-in-the-world. To live in clear-headed appreciation of the way of things, to live with proper pride in one's own being, requires us to face the certainty of our own deaths, and those of every other mortal thing. The very definition of 'living thing' includes its fate: the inanimate does not decay nor die

(although it may corrode, erode, dissolve, or dissipate)—
which is why Aristotle concluded that wind-eggs were living:
because they can go bad! Some have argued—perhaps a little
in the spirit of Aesop's Fox—that never-ending life would not
be worth having, although their arguments rest on nothing
more than fantasy: Makropoulos does not find her life worth
living, but that proves nothing (since she is a fantasy), and
does not even hint at more than Plato's point, that unending
life would be no benefit to the unvirtuous. Others have argued
that the chance of an heroic death redeems all sorrows of an
errant life, that death is what gives boundaries and shape to
what would otherwise be an unsightly mass.

> Only in silence the word,
> only in dark the light,
> only in dying life:
> bright the hawk's flight
> on the empty sky.
>
> (Leguin 1968: 7)

To all this, however apt in its own proper place, we may retort
that dying is not a game. The verse that Bridges rejected as a
cynical aberration contains a moral that all those who seek to
theorize of death should hold to heart:

> The shepherd's brow, fronting forked lightning,
> owns the horror and the havoc and the glory
> of it. Angels fall, they are towers, from heaven—a story
> of just, majestical and giant groans.
> But man—we, scaffold of score brittle bones;
> who breathe from groundlong babyhood to hoary
> age gasp; whose breath is our memento mori—
> what bass is *our* viol for tragic tones?
> He! Hand to mouth he lives, and voids with shame;
> and, blazoned in however bold the name,
> Man Jack the man is, just; his mate a hussy.
> And I that die these deaths, that feed this flame,
> that . . . in smooth spoons spy life's masque mirrored: tame
> my tempests there, my fire and fever fussy.
>
> (Hopkins 1970: 107; see 296 n.)

On the one hand, death could only be a tragedy if it were the
overthrow of one deserving better. To be 'righteously aggrieved'

if we should not be given the due of nobler animals, and to make a tragic opera of dying—as Epictetus too remarked (*Discourses* 4. 7. 15)—is to be a poor philosopher. Richard Weaver's description of 'the typical Southern farmer or millhand':

From his point of view there is nothing written in the original bill of things which says the substance of the world must be distributed equally. Nor was there anything, before modern advertizers availed themselves of the press and radio, to tell him that he is entitled to the best of everything. (Weaver 1987: 199 f.)

The same must be true for length of life: where all is gift, who may complain? On the other hand, and more painfully, the process of dying is not a dignified retreat or culminating stroke, but far more often a painful and humiliating collapse. Dying no more brings out the best in most of us than poverty or oppression, and it is no part of any true philosophy, nor any wish of mine, to pretend that death is romantic. Nor are the 'little deaths' of cognitive humility (a readiness to kill one's dear hypothesis), and of virtuous living (a readiness to forgo present pleasures for the sake of duty), that much like dying. Those are deliberate acts, self-chosen virtues, and may—at the time—seem death-like: but death itself is not an action, not a thing we do, even if we consent to its being done, or bring it on ourselves. The essence of dying is that it is done to us, that we cannot in thinking of death forget the sweep of material being that governs us. Dying is a forceful reminder of our status as 'a little pile of inert matter' (Weil 1987: 286). Pain is an intimation of what death is—not because all deaths are painful, but because all pains are deathly, all remind us of our feeble grasp on being.

It is possible, and maybe at times desirable, to cherish romantic fantasies of death: to speak of dying as of no more importance than rising from a feast that has begun to bore. 'The self of each of us is not anger or fear or desire just as it is not bits of flesh or fluids either, but is that with which we reason and understand' (Plutarch, *De Facie Lunae* 945ᵃ). That potentially pure intellect may disentangle itself from its involvement in the world of flesh, and be all the better for it. Its 'immortality' is its detachment from the passing show.

Alternatively—if what we are is simply flesh, all 'dyings' are no more than alterations in the outward shape of matter. The sense of selfhood 'we' residually feel is an illusion to be transcended in the sight of the 'real world'. The totality of things, which we can contemplate 'as through a cranny' (Boethius, *Consolatio* 3. 9. 8), is eternal fact, and we are intellectually united with it when we see it so. We can conceive our death, can leap beyond the limits of our world and think of a time when we shall have lived and live no longer, because we can grasp that world that is not our world only, but the World itself. The Last Men, in Stapledon's fable, pompously declare that they 'can look forward without dismay to the inevitable deterioration of all that they cherish most, to the death of [their] fair community, and to the extinction of the human spirit', and even to the likelihood that 'the last of Man should be a whine' (Stapledon 1963: 600).Which is like looking forward 'calmly' to the certainty that one will end up as a diseased and homicidal maniac—or yet more agonizingly, that one's children may. Let us not pretend a virtue, if it is one, higher than we can conceive, lest one day we be asked to act on it. Boethius had a right to speak as he did, for he wrote from prison and on the brink of being clubbed to death. We should remember Epictetus:

Watch yourself and see how you take the word—I do not say the word that your child is dead; how could you possibly bear that?—but the word that your oil is spilled, or your wine drunk up. Well might someone stand over you when you are in this excited condition and say simply, 'Philosopher, you talk differently in the schools; why are you deceiving us? Why, when you are a worm, do you claim that you are a man?' (*Discourses* 4. 1. 14 ff.)

Maybe some have achieved a fierce joy in the discovery that

> I am food, I am food, I am food!
> I am an eater of food!
> I am an eater of food!
> I am an eater of food!
> I who am food eat the eater of food!
> I have overcome the whole world!
> (*Taittiriya Upanishad*)

This thing here has its very existence in the ceaseless exchange of energies; it is a wave of the underlying sea. Eat and be eaten! But the realistic possibility of being killed and eaten produces something more than a delighted horror: imagine if you were yourself what Gollum had in mind in that most brilliant and beloved-of-children line: 'Is it nice, my preciousss? Is it juicy? Is it scrumptiously crunchable?'

I do not mean to deny that people may die 'well'. Some have lived so long, however long that is, that they would gladly sleep. Others are happy to conceive their own continuance in children, monuments, and others' memories. Others again expect to wake to life immortal and unwearying, the celestial butterflies who only dreamed they were people, and are only casually amused by abstract arguments that deny the chance. Not all of us will wish to live at any cost, and any may prefer to go down virtuously than to save a shattered life. The philosopher, so Epictetus said, may sometimes die rather than shave his beard, just as other saints and heroes have preferred to die rather than deny their life's meaning by offering a pinch of incense or eating a piece of pig. Few of us will unashamedly declare that mere continuance of sensual life is a worthwhile object. Most of us will agree that there are far worse things than simply dying, even in our prime. I do not know how many of us really would prefer death to dishonour; the fact that responses to those who do are so often contemptuous or puzzled or, at least, surprised does give us all some reason to doubt our own sincerity. Would we think it newsworthy that a man died to save his child, or any unrelated child, if we were confident that we would do the same? 'When we see a man bravely facing his own extinction we rehearse the greatest victory we can imagine' (Becker 1973: 12).

'The kind of man you are depends on the centre with which you identify yourself' (Warren 1964: 97), on the *skopos*, the goal, set deep inside your heart. Death and its prospect bring to light the diversity of goals between which we are torn, and the disparity between what we say we value and what we act to save. 'Where your treasure is, there shall your heart be'. Death brings the prospect closer that no goal we set up for ourselves here-now will hold our hearts or bodies. Death, all too often, is an humiliating collapse not merely of bodily function, but of good intentions. We had better all apologize beforehand.

What it is that Perishes

So the aphorism that death is not an event in life, not a thing we live through and so not a thing to be feared, is not entirely true, even if there is no celestial awakening. Dying is something we can expect to do, even if the end is silence, and even if we are asleep in the doing of it. To say that one should not rationally mind about death because one will not be there to complain can never be anything but a sophism: that one will not be there, that one will have been dissolved, 'as if one had never been', is exactly what we mind about. The sophism rests upon the unexamined claim that one cannot rationally now care about events that one will not care about once they have happened, even if the event one cares about is, exactly, the coming-about that one no longer cares. Any intellectual fears the future in which she shall have lost her mind, even if that future is of 'happy' idiocy; any lover loathes the thought that she may 'happily' cease to love. Both futures are deathly; death, if it is no awakening, is no less.

In the first volume I expressed some alarm at contemporary efforts to eliminate the fear of death: that fear, as Hobbes pointed out, is of more practical effect even than the fear of God, in helping to keep the peace. Those who really do not fear death are strictly incorrigible. There are no threats that can confine them: 'the door', as the Stoics said, 'is always open'. 'He who does not respect his life even in principle cannot be restrained from the most dreadful vices; he recks neither king nor torments' (Kant 1930: 153). But although philosophers should think carefully before multiplying the number of death-commandos it may still be true that the fear of death, however useful for the Queen's Peace, is somehow irrational. If the gods were invented for the state's security, as Critias declared, perhaps 'death' was too.

What is it whose end we fear? This flesh here-now will not, quite, end, even if it ceases to be flesh, any more than it ever, quite, began, except in the primeval monobloc itself: we were all that monobloc, when we were in that monobloc. Italo Calvino's poetry:

Naturally, we were all there,—old Qfwfq said,—where else could we have been? Nobody knew then that there could be space. Or time either: what use did we have for time, packed in there like sardines? I say 'packed like sardines', using a literary image: in reality there wasn't even space to pack us into. Every point of each of us coincided with every point of each of the others in a single point, which was where we all were. In fact, we didn't even bother one another, except for personality differences, because when space doesn't exist having somebody unpleasant like Mr Pber[t] Pber[d] underfoot all the time is the most irritating thing (Calvino 1969: 43)

—so now you know why space exists, though Calvino himself, more traditionally, ascribes the expansion that created space and time to an impulse of generosity on the part of Mrs Ph(i)Nk[o]: 'Oh, if only I had some room, the noodles I would make for you boys!'

Absurd, of course: consider it light relief.

In those days of the Dreamtime, let us fashionably suppose, there were no creatures to converse on anything or to identify their separate and enduring selves. The things here-now are materially continuous with that beginning. We can say of them, and of ourselves, that there is nothing there but their material constituents, formed in the first few seconds of the world, and packed since then into ever more complex knots by stellar furnaces. Every piece of us is star-stuff, and that stuff, if we analyse it long enough, turns out to be mere wave formations in the underlying space. The one 'substance' as traditionally conceived (which is to say the one thing that can subsist by itself and of which every change or chance is predicated) is what we had thought of as 'mere empty space'. Not only is our present material being continuous with the monobloc; it is a local modulation of a present being, no more to be accorded primitive status than the waves of the sea, or the shape of a fountain. When the world-amoeba stirs, 'we' speak, but it is no less silly to bewail the fate of such a piece of matter or such a local variation in the space-time curves than to wish to freeze the sea.

The One remains. The Many shift and pass.

Even the thought or fear of death is only a passing colour on the surface of things, of the one thing that there really is. There are no 'real' or 'fundamental' differences between the living, the dead, and the inanimate, and if all that is true, there can be nothing important that will end. The thing that is thought to die, on this view never 'lived', for 'it' does not exist as a real subject. Matter or Space-Time is the only Real Subject, and everything that seems real is only a qualification or disturbance or position of that One.

But perhaps, as Aristotle thought, it cannot be right to identify mere Matter (or Space-Time) with true Substance? Matter just as such, or Space-Time just as such, though everything is predicable of 'it', is not a real subject of predication, as if it were one real thing 'beneath' the many transformations, colourings, or shifts that constitute the world of our experience, 'the many million, million selves; ephemeridae, each to itself, the universe's one quick point, the crux of all cosmical endeavour' (Stapledon 1963: 605). We do not solve the emotional crisis occasioned by the prospect of dying by pretending that Stuff does not die: the horror of death just is that we are then assimilated to mere Stuff!

As an animal organism man senses the kind of planet he has been put down on, the nightmarish, demonic frenzy in which nature has unleashed billions of individual organismic appetites of all kinds— not to mention earthquakes, meteors and hurricanes, which seem to have their own hellish appetites. Each thing in order to deliciously expand, is forever gobbling up others. (Becker 1973: 54).

One can certainly say that 'that bit of stuff is George', and continue to do so even when George is dead and cremated, but this is, in Aristotelian terms, an 'accidental predication', true only because it is true that George is (was) made of stuff. The point here is that there can be no real class of 'bits of stuff' concerning which we could ever hope to formulate properly scientific generalizations, ones that identified real causes. 'Bits of stuff' is as inane a class as 'mauve things over three feet high whose name in Cherokee begins with K or S', or 'harries' (Boler 1963: 27). Doubtless there are or might be such things, but there is no one syndrome that guarantees that they be mauve or over three feet high still less that some arbitrary

label for them begin with K. In order to have scientific
understanding of what there is we need to identify real classes,
and real closures.

What Aristotle suggested, accordingly, was that Form must
constitute Substance: what something was, its being the sort
of thing it was, was not the selfsame matter as just any other
thing. There are distinct substances, by any normal account,
which are not all just one sort of thing, suitably coloured in.
Being 'a bit of matter' is not being anything in particular, and
we have no grasp of what such matter might be except
through our grasp of the way real, present things begin, decay,
or change. The bronze ball that once was a bronze statue and
will soon be many souvenirs from Rhyl is now a distinct
subject, not just bronze in one particular location: or rather,
for such artificial examples are not quite convincing, Miss T.
is distinct from what she eats, even if there are also identifiable
things that being now coterminous with her once were not,
and will not be in the future. The identity of any present thing
is given by the form that informs the various matters variously
and temporarily involved. The statue is not in the end a good
example, precisely because its 'being a statue' plays very little
part in any causal story. Statues are not a natural kind.

Identity as any particular thing is not given by the bits and
pieces it may share with past or future things, but by the
present organizing principles that briefly maintain it against
the dark.

> As bodies change, and as I do not weare
> those Spirits, humors, blood I did last yeare,
> and, as if on a streame I fixe mine eye,
> that drop, which I looked on, is presently
> pusht with more waters from my sight, and gone,
> so in this sea of vertues, can no one
> bee'insisted on; vertues, as rivers, passe,
> yet still remains that vertuous man there was
>
> (Donne 1929: 235 f.)

So it is not unreasonable to say, after all, that the form, and so
the identity, of this thing here has not been from the
beginning. We were not all There in the first singularity, for
'we' are those things organized according to the principles

appropriate to our sort of thing, a sort that could not really have inhabited no-space. Our matter, suitably described, began back there, but we did not. Our matter, suitably described, will outlast time, but we shall not.

Unfortunately, even this does not quite give us common sense results. If what matters in me, what makes me one thing and not another and so defines my boundaries in time and space, is the organizing principles at work here-now, 'I' am immune to death, for they may outlast what 'normally' I would consider Me. An organizing principle, after all, is precisely a system of subsystems working with a host of others, and perhaps subsumed in larger systems. The form of this thing here, let us suppose, is compounded of the instructions embodied in its DNA (at one level), and in its chemically recorded memories, its RNA. Not that the Form just is those chemicals, any more than this set of sentences just is the lights on my computer screen, the magnetic markers on the disc, the black traces on a piece of paper or the sound-waves in a lecture-hall. All those other systems may, on occasion, embody the sentences, which are themselves encoded instructions to my hearers' or readers' RNA. There are some limits on the sort of chemicals that could serve as the immediate material of such a commanding Form, but the complex of genetic and individual programs is not identical even with those chemicals. In possible worlds or possible futures just the same instructions might be encoded otherwise.

So two things follow: first that such coded programs cannot work just 'by themselves'. The instructions for the growth of one human creature are entirely useless if there are not also other programs at work to provide the right environment, not merely in the womb but in the world at large. They cannot work if there are not also instructions hidden in the program, for the growth of all the complex symbiotes that share what 'we' self-centredly consider 'ours'. Each of us is a colony organism, embedded in a biosphere and universe that has a larger program than just 'ours'. To put the matter rhetorically: just as my liver is an essential part of 'me' because 'I' cannot survive without it, so also are the algae on the shore without which I (and you) would die of sulphur loss. It is impossible to conceive of human beings that long inhabit an otherwise 'dead' world, just as we cannot conceive that they would long exist without their kidneys, lungs, or spinal cord.

So to speak of 'me here-now' is to imagine a boundary between Me and Not-me that we cannot seriously or exactly draw: some things, no doubt, are things I can live well enough without, but the living earth is not one of them! Conceive yourself as a set of concentric circles: how narrowly you draw the circles, or how widely, has no one reasonable answer. Maybe to lose your leg, your arm, your eyes makes no essential difference in you, whereas the loss of mind or morals may. But what if you lose those lungs outside your skin, the tropical rain-forests or the mid-ocean plankton? Or what if civilization crumbles, and you wake to Auden's nightmare?

> A ragged urchin, aimless and alone,
> loitered about that vacancy, a bird
> flew up to safety from his well-aimed stone:
> that girls are raped, that two boys knife a third,
> were axioms to him, who'd never heard
> of any world where promises were kept,
> or one could weep because another wept.
>
> (Auden 1966: 295)

I said 'you wake': but such a waking could hardly be of what any of us now conceive to be our whole, true self. There are moral equivalents of death, or worse.

Again, just as 'statues' are not a natural kind, not a class such that every member has the selfsame nature, is caused in the same way and has identical relationships with other things, so neither are 'human beings'. Humankind, if it is equated with the species *Homo sapiens*, turns out not to be a kind in the old sense at all. This thing here-now is a member of that species merely as being a member of an historically identifiable population, of creatures biologically related to the sample few. A type-specimen in modern biological terms is not a creature that exemplifies the 'real form' of the species, such that others are its conspecifics by 'resembling' it—though this notion still crops up amongst philosophers. The likely resemblances between conspecifics may be diagnostic, but they are not the essence of conspecificity, any more than the marked resemblances between blood members of the

'Oswestry Clark family' are what make them members. They resemble each other because they are related: they are not related because they resemble each other. Whales feed their young with mother's milk because they are mammals; they are not mammals because they feed their young with milk. This alteration in our conception of conspecificity has enormous implications, which I have partly explored in Clark 1988*c*, my contribution in absentia to the World Archaeological Congress of 1986. What is important here is that being the thing (the human thing) I am cannot be detached from my being related to a host of other things. For there to be one man there must be a biosphere, and a vast congregation of co-operating humans, hominids, mammals, vertebrates, and, generally, animalia. One swallow does not make a species, and so is not a swallow.

I must go further: if being the sort of thing I am rests in the co-operating programs of so many things, and what I am here-now is the expression of such programs as reach out wider than my flesh, and will last longer, does it not follow that what is important in 'being me' may last in children, nieces, and the evolving population from which I take my name? What right have modernists to scorn the 'primitive' judgement that the young Taugwalder, now grown old, 'is' old Father Taugwalder (Duerr 1985: 116, *contra* Gellner)? Perhaps not all the elements and subsystems of those programs will come together again in quite the way that they do now, but why should that concern me? The programs that co-operatively make this here will make much the same things there, even if, as it were, my putative grandson has my nose, my great-niece has my eyes, and no one till the seventh generation thinks like me. 'I' shall be scattered through the population. In fact it does not even much matter whether I have children: practically nothing of what makes up me will be a unique mutation (and what *is* is probably a trivial matter).

This doctrine you will recognize as one that has obtained some notoriety in recent years, though mostly among those who enjoy sneering at others' hopes and beliefs without themselves giving any real thought to what it implies. We are, it is said, survival machines unconsciously programmed by the DNA or RNA we carry: genes and memes together rule the world, outlasting all the vehicles they make to serve their turn. Those who make this an absolutely general thesis, of course, imply that their own advocacy of the theory is gene-led. Neo-Darwinians will leave more offspring in the long run than Fundamentalists, perhaps. Such moral philosophers, including myself, as have attended to the wilder claims of socio-biologists to derive ethics from evolutionary calculation, have usually observed that this is to confuse explanation and justification. Even if it were demonstrably the case that we had the moral qualms or principles we do because having such qualms or principles had given our ancestors an evolutionary edge over those who did not, it would not follow that those principles were justified as tactical devices for propagating our own genes, as if that were our primary goal. It is not, as such, our goal at all, nor anything else's. If it pleases us to believe that in a million years our genes will dominate the population descended from the present human species this can only be because we wish the things we value to be valued still.

But though the idea of remodelling our 'moral system' so that our genes may dominate some descendant population is, at first glance, ridiculous, there is a truth concealed. 'Everything possible to be believ'd is an image of the truth', and 'the law of loyalty to one's kind, one's kindred' is one axiom of natural morality. In so far as 'what I am' is a complex of co-operating programs that are also at work outside my skin and will be so in ages past my sight, then the inbuilt impulse to preserve oneself, that *conatus* which Spinoza, following Aristotle, identified with the real being of each apparent individual (3p17: 1982: 109; see Clark 1983: 99), must issue in an identical concern for the *same nature* everywhere.

This is indeed the point which Spinoza made the centre of his ethics: every thing that has a being at all endeavours to persevere in it, which is to say, endeavours to maintain that program's grip upon the world. 'The natural striving of the creature goeth towards distinctiveness, fighteth against primeval, perilous sameness. This is called the *principium individuationis*' (Jung's *Sermons*, cited by Singer 1973: 330). Non-rational creatures do this unknowingly: parents die for their offspring, social insects for their nest, without intending any such result. Rational beings can recognize the same program, the same nature, in their fellows and come to see that self-preservation amounts to universal (intellectual) love. This thing here may perish, but its value even to itself is as an actualization of an abiding form. Spinoza's ethical egoism becomes a humanism because he fails to recognize the self-same nature, or many elements of it, in creatures more distantly related to us. He would not, of course, have fallen as far as Lewis's Weston, who cannot see a common humanity, cannot see the *hnau*, in alien or savage guise, and readily abuses those concrete manifestations that he does see in the name of an abstract, unknown future. Spinozistic ethics, ill-understood, have played a part in the development of the scientific world's neglect of ethical questions about the use of 'animals', but only a few alterations in the Spinozistic system are required to allow for our recognition of our complicity with dogs, whales, bees, or aliens. Anywhere at all that the world has turned round upon itself to make creatures that co-operate and seek to understand is a place that the form of me is working: 'I am human, and nothing at all is alien to me', to rework the tag.

There is some evidence that I am not simply making up a system. Science Fiction writers, and their readers, clearly get great pleasure from the imagining of distant futures, possible worlds where humankind has evolved out into space, carrying with it the genetic and cultural heritage that now defines us all. Some have depicted futures where some substantial part of the program that governs, for example, this twentieth-century free-range academic might be preserved or reconstructed so as to run a seventieth-century space explorer. Writers and readers alike know well that things will not be as they are imagined here: the details of the vision do not count. What influences this distant view is our emotional attachment to the moving form of things.

'If our universe is a complex living structure then every one of our actions has consequences in its remotest parts', and death is never an end (Jang Dongsun, 1886–1965, quoted by Elvin 1985: 183). Whatever things are like, there will be some abiding truths: spring will return and, symbolically, the swallow. Terror enters the picture when we try to conceive an end, an end not only of this organism here (which is only the form's vehicle) but of all humanly recognizable being. This is Schell's point (1982: 155): the death of one human organism is balanced by the survival of humankind; even the death of humankind at large would be balanced by the survival of the biosphere from which it springs; the final death, if such there could be, would be the end of all the great experiment.

Haecceitas and Hopkins

So neither Matter nor Form (or at any rate, abstract Form) appears to identify whatever it is that, as individuals, we fear to lose, or fear will be lost. Materially, this thing here-now is of one stuff with everything else, and cannot end. As far as nature goes, nothing ever dies, but is only transformed.[1] Its being 'one' bit or 'many' is not in the end important. All counting operations, after all, are relative to the current purpose of the counters. Formally, this thing here-now is the construct of an unimaginably vast system of subsystems, that have made like things long ago, and will again. Consider the flames of Stapledon's fable: counting how many flames there are, or identifying when one flame is at last extinguished (given that they can sleep in the dust of the air for aeons), is an impossible task. The fable, you will recall, includes the rule that sudden drenchings in cold water may put out the flame— but one flame's memories and purposes are still reflected in its siblings' lives—and how exactly is that different from its reflection in one follower flame that could be called 'the same'? We may believe it easy enough, for example, to count how many people are now here, and say when they are 'dead', but slower organisms might still have doubts. Multiple selves and stages, reincarnating spirits, are not wild hypotheses, but simply ways of speaking of our common condition.

In the language of the Neoplatonic system which I am

---

[1] Philo LA 1. 7: 1929: i. 151 cites Euripides fr. 839: 'nothing that is born doth die: its severed parts together fly, and yield another shape.'

slowly expounding in these three volumes: matter, 'star-stuff', is the mirror within which the forms ceaselessly reflect themselves. It may seem to us here-now that localized individual things are the true reality, that their shared properties are only 'likenesses' that 'we' choose to remember. But the truth is rather that the Forms are perpetually mirrored in, or shape, the star-stuff. Particulars may perish, but only because star-stuff moves on, or the forms of life 'withdraw'.

And yet we are afraid. It may be good to remember our material continuity, to awaken in ourselves the sense that the constituent elements of these our bodies run back through geological epochs to exploding stars and to the monobloc. It may be good to remember that the forms that shape us have a wider life than this, and that 'we' shall be remembered and reflected and reproduced in the whole living world until our remotest selves and descendants leave the evaporated universe behind and travel through worm-holes to another lively dimension! Or else, of course, be lost. If our selfhood is what we strive to preserve, and what we strive to preserve is our goal, our project, then we may gladly or resignedly give our flesh to serve that thing.

> Each mortal thing does one thing and the same:
> deals out that being indoors each one dwells;
> selves—goes itself; myself it speaks and spells,
> crying what I do is me: for that I came.
>
> (Hopkins 1970:90)

What a thing *is* is what it aims at, as Aristotle too suggested (see Clark 1983:ch. 3.3). 'All souls being all things, each will be differentiated according to its operative phase, which in turn is determined by the object of each soul's vision' (O'Daly 1973: 24, after *Ennead* 4. 3. 8, 12). But this reflected or projected being can only be what Hopkins called a 'sake':

I mean by it the being a thing has outside itself, as a voice by its echo, a face by its reflection, a body by its shadow, a man by his name, fame or memory, and also that in the thing by virtue of which especially it has this being abroad, and that is something distinctive, marked, specifically or individually speaking, as for a voice and echo clearness; for a reflected image light, brightness; for a shadow casting body bulk; for a man of genius, great achievements, amiability, and so on. (Letter to Robert Bridges, cited by Cotter 1972: 199).

The being a thing has 'outside itself', which might perhaps be what the Egyptians intended by its 'ka', is no small matter, but does not of itself identify what it is that that thing individually fears the loss of (though it may be a clue to it).

There is another way of seeing those abiding forms, and one which—if you have followed me so far—you may already have suspected. What they are are gods. There are abiding presences and principles within the living world, which do not need any particular mortal votary. When spring returns, and the swallow, it is the lady Aphrodite renewing her covenant. When men go to war, in Arnhem or before the walls of Troy, they can endure it only because the gods of war breathe power into their falling limbs. I do not mean, remember, that there are such persons as those gods that we might meet on board the Starship *Enterprise*, as if they were extraterrestrial bandits. The gods (or demons) are not persons like ourselves: they are immortal moods, modes, possibilities that we can represent to ourselves in stories, rituals, and conversations. That they are immortal precisely identifies the difference: 'we' are not. We lose the thread of argument, fall in and out of love, experience collapse and divided loyalties, fear death.

On the one hand, what we are is the complex form we choose out from all possibilities, the gods we serve in their due order, what will be our 'nature'. 'My life is a diversity of relationships with them' (Hillman 1975: 35). On the other hand, such singleness of spirit is not ours 'by nature' and the goal of our endeavours, simply in that it may outlast us, is not quite we. Duns Scotus long before the existentialists, as I reported in an earlier chapter: 'Self before nature is no thing as yet but only possible; with the accession of a nature it becomes properly a self, for instance a person' (cited by Hopkins 1959a: 148). The uncatchable self that wills a nature, serves an immortal, instantiates a form, is what death illuminates. The presence of Truth, of which I wrote before, is experienced in the sheer particularity of any mortal things, and most especially in the knowledge that it is I shall die. 'The final terror of self-consciousness is the knowledge of one's own death' (Becker 1973: 70): but perhaps the latter knowledge comes first.

The inhabitants of Planet 8, in Lessing's fable (1982), are compelled to face the death of everything that breathes upon their world, and to see that, for example, the charm, the friendliness, the quickness of a dead beast (or of themselves) is not confined to that, and long survives it. The god, the functional identity, of each of them must also live, whether it is Keeper of Animals, or Fruit Maker, Midwife, Doctor, Writer. But who or what is I, in each of them:

Doeg tells tales and sings songs in all times and places, everywhere people use sounds to communicate, so if I am no longer Doeg, then Doeg still is, and perhaps as the dark comes down we are looking as we raise our eyes at worlds where Doeg is at work, for Doeg has to be. But who am I, and what is my name? (Lessing 1982: 109).

It is that I, 'this consciousness, here I am, this is I, this is me, this sensation that I cannot communicate to anyone' (Lessing 1982: 82), which fears an end, that sees a possible limit to its stay. But there is a final paradox: each of us knows that feeling very well. 'This little feeling, here I am, the feeling of me . . . is not mine at all, but is shared, it must be'. The most particular and private sense of self-identity is shared, who knows by how many? 'I AM is uttered in ten thousand places' (Cotter 1972: 129 after Hopkins 1970: 90). Lessing here imitates, with more success and literary skill, a novel of Stapledon's where a bomber crew gradually awaken upward through successive steps to know the Atman that looked out through all their eyes (and their enemies': 1946). It is that which can fear its death, and at the same time realize its own immunity. 'I', whatever that is that knows the taste of 'me' in everything and knows its own dependence, is not what had been thought. This organism here is a colony, or a fragment, or a vehicle for passing and indifferent gods: 'I', if it names anything, names that consciousness which each such organism hugs to itself.

Each one of us is a package of hearts, livers, kidneys, entrails, bones, and each one of these is a whole and knows itself. A heart knows it is a heart and feels itself to be that. And so with a liver and every other thing inside every animal, inside you. You are a parcel, a package of smaller items, wholes, entities, each one feeling its identity, saying to itself, Here I am! just as you do in moments of sensing what you are. (Lessing 1982: 62 f.)

And conversely, one may say to 'Canopus', which is Lessing's label for an enlightened vision:

You look at us all and see not the swarming myriads, but sets of wholes, as we, looking into the waters of our lake, or up into the skies, saw there groups and swarms and schools and flocks, each consisting of a multitude of individuals thinking themselves unique, but each making, as we would see with our superior supervising eyes, a whole, an entity, moving as one. (1982:83)

Colonies and colonies of colonies make up the cosmos 'each to itself the universe's one quick point', and each—in a way—correct.

The individual of our present moral consciousness is the valuable thing that maybe perishes, the irreplaceable identity that may perform many functions in the social or the physical world, and finds or makes its 'nature' just in what it does—'crying what I do is me: for that I came'. One error open to revisionists, I think, is to eliminate that bare identity. Perhaps, as may often seem reasonable, there is nothing else than form and matter to consider. Maybe it is absurd to think that there is something else than projects, memories, and personalities to be valued. Maybe it should be fully acknowledged that each organism here is a segment of a larger whole, a single experiment of the enduring species. Findlay, describing the Wittgensteinian revolution, declared that there was 'no sense of "same" which corresponds more closely with the "nature of things" than any other', and that this was—by implication—a *welcome* 'charter of freedom' (Findlay 1963: 30). But if it is, what can be said against a re-evaluation of our moral code? Maybe some such theorists have concluded to a 'liberal' moral, for example, not to punish for a past self's error. But the principle that each should bear the burden of her own iniquity took shape within a metaphysic that drew radical distinctions between one self and another. Once that distinction is a superstition, why should we resist the 'illiberal' model, that what we call children should be punished for their parents' wrongs, or whole populations razed for one member's fault? If it is no more 'realistic' to identify me as 'the same person' as past Stephens than as 'the same flesh' as past Clarks, or as 'a different day-self' from yesterday's, or as 'the same soul' as, arbitrarily, this body's maternal grandfather, what defends liberal individualism? That is indeed the practical effect of certain self-styled liberal reformers, who berate whole families for one member's 'madness', or imprison children because their fathers might have done some wrong.

Morality, in more than the bare minimum of social order, wakens when an individual sees that hitting others is just the same as being hit: for 'me', to beat up 'you' and 'you' to beat up 'me' are just the same. And conversely, my irreplaceability, my value, is known indirectly through the sudden or gradual conviction that another is thus infinitely valued. If individuals were only instances of some, however complex, form, they would in principle, and often in practice, be replaceable. Lovers could be quite satisfied to have another version of the once-beloved. Adolescents to whom I put the case usually say that 'yes, they would'! But that is because such adolescents have not woken up to sense the bare identity behind the passing show: beloveds, to them, are only objects, not the same self as they (see Marcel 1951: i. 48).

'I', Atman, looks out of every creature, even those who cannot say the word. Or if it does not, and this whole conviction is, like religion, a 'disease of language', it must be concluded that the skeins and segments of the human species, or the biosphere, 'we' had thought were 'us' are simply bearers of immortal values. If all that is meant by 'conscious' is 'alert', and all that is meant by 'I' is this thing here, what value has alertness or locality? 'Things that alertly localize themselves', or processes that issue in such acts, are of a piece with rolling rocks and swarming butterflies, to be remade if so it suits the masters. I had rather believe Plutarch.

7

Two Natures, One Identity

Dualism, Dissonance

I wrote in the last chapter of philosophy as the practice of death, the serious attempt to think away from worldly or bodily cares, and of what it was that was known in the thought of its own possible destruction, the thing that was neither form nor matter, but the Self itself. But there was another image for philosophy amongst the ancients: Penelope, undoing by night what she had woven by day. It is the essence, some would say, of true philosophy that no theories are left standing as the only truth, or even as any truth at all. What we weave in our daytime being we must unweave by night. The Lady Philosophy often looks like the angel of the Tarot pack, labelled Temperance, who is pouring water from one flask to the other, and then pouring it back again. Even if there is, as Boethius and Peirce both hoped, a Truth that is 'one, without a flaw', we do not now possess it, and must often be content to maintain two, three, or many theories that each in their turn seem plausible, even though we cannot see how they should fit together. To maintain them, or to hold them lightly, or withhold all final assent.

Which has at least two morals. First, that we should always allow the still small voice that whispers 'Fiddlesticks!' (Wallas 1926: 117, after W. K. Clifford) its own authority, and so be ready to check or controvert even our most precious theories. Maybe 'his own thinking is of all things the dearest to every man of liberal thinking and a philosophical tendency' (T. L. Peacock, *Headlong Hall*, ch. 14), and maybe there is a case even for the aphorism that 'truth is that which a man troweth . . . (and) thus the truth of one man is not the truth of another' (ch. 7). That is at any rate an improvement on the social idealist's dogma that truth is what 'a society'—or rather its established sages—'troweth'. What it is I am here-now is identified in the goal and system that informs my doings. But the practice of death does require that this little truth be abandoned or demoted. 'The picture of the world which was born at a man's birth . . . that which he does not invent but rather discovers within himself, (that) is himself over again, his being expressed in words' (Spengler 1926: i. p. xiii), is a picture or fragmentary experiment that must take second place to that Real World which is the world devised or contemplated by the Self of all things. And so the very picture I have just sketched must be a myth, or partial truth, to be transcended in a higher, dialectic vision.

The second, contrary, moral to be drawn from my opening remarks is that the necessary demonstration of inconsistency is not always reason to dismiss that inconsistent theory. It may be, as I said, that there are many occasions when we can do no better than to offer two or more accounts, each useful and even absolute upon occasion, which we cannot consistently imagine. There is a strange inconsistency in, for example, Vickers' comparison of 'occult' and 'experimentalist' mentalities (1984): on the one hand, occult or animistic thought aims to include everything within a single system, while experimentalists are content to leave much unexplained or only partly modelled; on the other, occult thinkers are unimpressed by contradictions experimentalists seek to eliminate. My own judgement is that any sensible theorist, of whatever tradition, tolerates an indefinable amount of dissonance, even while hoping for, but not now enjoying, a unitary theory. Indeed, the very moment when it becomes clear that there is no one identifiable fault to be found with a popular theory is that at which, being completed, that theory must be transcended.

Which brings me to the topic of this chapter. The title is intended to remind the well-informed of Chalcedonian orthodoxy, its problems and its possible merits: how can there be one entity, one individual, that is identically both God and Man? The issue is not unrelated to the one that I have set myself to understand, or at least expound, but it is not my present topic. I will so far indulge myself here-now as to say that in my view the issue is commonly misstated: there is in fact no problem whatsoever in supposing that one thing, the Word of God, should be both God and Man. To suppose that there is is to have misunderstood what sort of thing the Word of God might be! That Word and Wisdom, as Philo of Alexandria taught, is at once the means of creation and the form of Humanity (*De Spec. Leq.* 4. 12). That Heavenly Humanity is the Tree of Life, to be contrasted with the second man, who is of the earth, earthy (*De Plantatione* 44). Paul, you will remember, suggested that the Lord from Heaven came second in the temporal order (1 Corinthians 15: 47 f.). That is one interesting innovation in mainstream Christianity which makes it different from mainstream Neoplatonism: that the Word is not simply Man, but is identical with a particular man. It is its particularity, not its nature, that is shocking, though even non-Christian Neoplatonists did in fact allow for the taking-up of some particular example of humanity into the Godhead. *Pace* Dunn, Philo's Heavenly Man, the *Logos*, is not 'a bloodless idea, a passive prototype and model' to be contrasted in a clear way with 'a personal divine being' (1980: 56).

But all that is by the way, until another volume. My present concern is with the notion sometimes offered as a parallel or metaphor for the Chalcedonian orthodoxy, namely that any human person is both a reasonable soul and human flesh. How can this thing be? Or what is the relation between the inner self, the consciousness that all but behaviourists admit to, and the bodily being whose motions the more optimistic neurophysiologists may hope to comprehend?

The merely simple-minded ('monophysite'!) response (and the one that modernists have begun to reckon axiomatic) is that the human person is the unitary subject of both mentalistic and physical properties. A human being can be characterized as 'six-feet tall, brown-haired and weighing ten stone' and also as 'believing that Plato wrote the Seventh Letter, being pathologically afraid of mice and hoping for promotion'. Those latter attributes can be given merely functional interpretations, in terms of what that human subject does or might do, says or might say—though it is by no means clear that either 'doing' or 'saying' is as merely 'behavioural' a notion as those functionalists suppose. Neither physical nor mentalistic attributes, so described, are ones the creature would have had outside all language (an issue to which I shall return in the third and final volume), and all are attributes that other creatures than their subject can discern. I am not the only good witness (and am sometimes no good witness at all) about my hopes, beliefs, and fears, any more than I alone know just how tall I am. Nor is there one thing that is happy, fearful, hopeful, meditating war, or calculating arithmetical results ('the soul'), and quite another that is talking, sighing, waving its fists, or chewing its pen. As Aristotle emphasized, it is not the soul that weaves or waves its fists, any more than any other part or discriminable aspect does (as, for example, the brain), but the whole human person (*De Anima* 1. 408^b 11). It is I that speaks or writes or meditates, and 'I' must mean a single entity causally responsible for the physical changes mentioned there.

It always astonishes classicists that theologians so often seem to think that there is a distinctively Hebrew notion of the whole person, with both physical and mentalistic properties, to be distinguished from the 'Greek' mistake of dual substances, body and soul unfirmly yoked. The error is often associated with the equally misleading attempt to distinguish Hellenic and Hebraic elements in the doctrine of Christ's person. In the first place, very few Greeks accepted 'Pythagorean' or 'Orphic' or 'Platonic' doctrine on the subject, preferring to believe, like other people, that they knew what they were, and that that was—what everyone said they were. In the second place, Platonic or Pythagorean dissatisfaction with our present worldly state, which is hardly a neurotic foible, does not involve a dualism of substance. It issues in familiar images, of 'the soul' that masters 'the body', or the body that is the soul's prison or tomb or slave. But the conviction that we are not really what we now sense ourselves to be is not, in Platonic context, a belief that there really are two things, two genuine subjects yoked to make one human person. What we miscall 'the body' is not a real subject, because it is not a real substance. The complex phenomenal body is not the real thing, but only 'a portion of the Soul discern'd by the five Senses, the chief inlets of the Soul in this age' (Blake 1966: 149). 'The Soul' or *Psuche* is simply Plato's name for that which must be in good order if the whole person is to be happy and healthy. Socrates (Plato, *Charmides* 156 D ff.) attributes to the Thracian god Zalmoxis the view that Greek physicians were failing to practice a properly holistic medicine that takes account of the soul's state, whether it is good or evil. Body, as Robinson observes, is part of the soul (1970: 5), not a separate thing, a corpse untidily united with a living spirit.

But I said that it was merely simple-minded to conclude that human subjects or persons had both physical and mentalistic properties, that it was of the nature of humanity to be thus diverse. It is still more so to insist, without the slightest attempt to ferret out or analyse dissenting doctrines, that 'all human societies' have a shared belief in just such human subjects as real, ultimate, or indissoluble. The truth is that we do not know whether all human, let alone all rational, societies have any such 'shared solid core' of belief in just those human subjects understood as spatially locatable, temporally reidentifiable, physically explicable, countable substances. 'Descriptive metaphysics', purporting to describe such a solid core of doctrine, is rarely more than armchair anthropology, and does not—in my judgement—even describe the single structure of 'our' world, let alone the worlds of archaic Greeks, or Amerindians, or first-century Graeco-Aramaeans! There is, as I have pointed out before, no one abstract answer to the question, how many subjects are there in this room, any more than to the question, how many things are there. Why then assume that all human societies will give the same answer?

But why am I characterizing single subject theories, as so far described, as simple-minded? First, for the reason just given: 'how many subjects?' is as ill-defined a question as 'how many things?', and the answers to be given are crucially dependent on the particular purpose of the questioner, the long-term assumptions of the answerer. Remember the comment that I cited in the second chapter: self-knowledge is like looking into a mirror and seeing the demons peering over one's shoulder! Their name is Legion.

But there is also a second reason to think that single-subject theories are somewhat simple-minded. They are characteristically offered in response to dualist suspicions: it is not that 'the body' has some properties and 'the soul' has others, but that the person is both physical and mental, accurately describable in both physicalist and mentalistic modes. It is sometimes suggested that the former mode involves description from the 'outside' (or objectively), and the latter description from the 'inside' (or empathetically). But as an answer to a metaphysical puzzle this is no more than evasion. Single-subject theories always seem to end up as materialistic ones. What we are confronted by is a situation where 'we' seem to be both straightforwardly physical, part of the grand sweep of material being to be explained according to just the same principles as any other material object, and also straight-forwardly subjective, individual agencies whose actions make sense under mentalistic concepts of intention, belief, desire, or dread. Simple assertion that there is one thing which is both physical and psychical ignores a host of problems. These are sometimes concealed from view by careful redirection: some concepts of 'folk-psychology', as moderns sometimes call our habit of ascribing desires, beliefs, feelings, emotions, percep-tions, and sensations to things like 'us', can be identified with 'scientifically' assessible syndromes. 'Getting the old adrenalin going' can easily enter folk psychology as a synonym for those processes that our predecessors knew as invocation of a patron spirit. As Walker has pointed out, Renaissance magic involves the creation of a demon by words sung in a special manner, a manner that gathers emotion, feeling tone, and thoughts together, and makes it possible to think and see things that one would not think in a different mood, possessed by a different demon (1958: 70). Vickers (1984: 118) is disturbed by Walker's readiness to take this sort of thing seriously (and would doubtless be appalled by Yeats, who invented a similar form of magic for himself), but it seems to me to be a mere description of actual and even ordinary experience—unless faulty conceptions of what it is to be a demon are brought into play.

But if you too are disturbed by that way of speaking, consider Midgley's judgement: 'some of us have to hold a meeting every time we want to do something only slightly difficult, in order to find the self who is capable of undertaking it' (1984: 123). And consider Ornstein's dictum:

Instead of a single, intellectual entity that can judge many different kinds of events equally, the mind is diverse and complex. It contains a changeable conglomeration of different kinds of 'small minds'—fixed reactions, talents, flexible thinking—'wheeled into consciousness'—and then usually discarded, returned to their place, after use. (Ornstein 1986: 25).

These small minds (or demons), once wheeled in may be difficult to dislodge—or to put it differently, we too often respond to events under the influence of stories that we actually know to be false. Ornstein cites one experimental result:

People were asked to read information that was very damaging to a public figure. Their attitude toward the person was measured before and after they read the material. Afterward, of course, their attitude changed in a negative direction. They they were told that the information they had read was a mistake; it was not about that public figure at all and had been made up. Their attitudes were again assessed, and they were still more negative to the public figure than when the study began. And the change persisted for weeks! (Ornstein 1986: 11)

All that is puzzling about Ornstein's story to a traditionalist like myself is that he seems to think that he thereby contradicts tradition, and that the computer metaphor he deploys to describe the situation actually helps our understanding of it. He does quote the occasional Sufi as showing precocious insight into human psychology, but appears to think such observations quite unprecedented. The modern habit of supposing that philosophy began with Descartes has a lot to answer for! The computer age has given us new metaphors for the diversity of spirit, involving subprograms and data stores that must be accessed if the whole is to perform, but the subjectively experienced process still involves invocation. The new metaphors are sometimes mistaken for novel insights and realistic explanations—but you may by now have gathered that my overall thesis just is that moderns have forgotten how complex and how careful our predecessors were. Though they urged us to follow the Way of Truth, of obedience to intellect, they were not so foolish as to suppose that this was easy. Integrity and right reason is our goal, and not our natural state. That they described our common human experience in terms of demons while modern psychologists prefer to think of neurophysiological events is not necessarily to their discredit. The charge that Vickers makes against the occult tradition, that they mistook their own metaphors for literal truths—which is a difficult charge to analyse—could be made with equal force against moderns.

Mind and Body

Where Aristotle analysed anger as a boiling of the blood informed by a desire for revenge (*De Anima* 1, 403^a 29), we can attain a higher physiological accuracy in the identification of hormones, tightened sphincter muscles, shifting electro-cerebral discharges. But we thereby neglect at least two things: first, that Aristotle did indeed include 'a desire for revenge' as the determining feature of one's anger; and, secondly, that not all mentalistically identifiable events can conceivably be identified with any physical events at all.

To take the second point first:

There are events we can deny only at astonishing expense of energy, as that my head aches. That ache may reflect or inform me of disturbances in the circulation of blood through my head, or of the need for sleep, or of the dangers of past and possible exertion. But the ache is not identical with any of those things of which it is, for me, a sign or symptom. For the ache is something essentially and forever painful (in all possible worlds where it exists at all it hurts), whereas there is no state of my brain or blood or muscle that is thus essentially painful. Either we can fully understand the brain-state R without referring to the pain to which (sometimes and some how) it 'gives rise', or we cannot. If we can, then the ache is something other than that physical condition; if we cannot, then such brain-states already have properties that are not mentioned in any physics textbook and that cannot be twisted into such 'physical' properties. All genuinely physical properties, I should point out, form part of a single system such that quantifiable energy can be exchanged between the different modes: pressure, temperature, and volume are equatable. Painfulness and heat are not—unless anyone wishes to suggest that one could warm a room up by first giving oneself a headache and then transposing the energy involved, or that wishes themselves are horses?

These very familiar arguments—well known to William James—leave us with several imaginable theories: first, that pains and other such compellingly real events are sheerly epiphenomenal, mere products (somehow) of the physical transformations that they shadow; second, that they are to be thought away, illusions of folk psychology; third, that 'being painful' and the like will eventually prove to be strictly deducible from the known physical natures of the things concerned; fourth, that they are what they indefeasibly seem, real events to be understood only 'from within', as elements of a mentalistic world. The arguments are very familiar, and not to be answered by glib appeals to 'systemic properties of the whole brain', or 'self-reflexive computers'. The bold attempt to do away not merely with mentalistic language but with the events we characterize as mental can convince no one: if it were adequate to our situation there would be no one to be convinced, and no moments of conviction. But if such things are real, then they are either inexplicable additions to the furniture of a physically determinable universe or else we must show that they can be understood as intelligibly grounded elements of a real world. The former appeal to inexplicability, or magic, is often dignified by talk of 'emergence', but in the absence of any other convincing example of emergence this should be seen as mere obfuscation. All the examples devised by commentators like Searle turn out to be simply further cases of the emergence, precisely, of the mental: 'liquidity' as a property of water which is neither possessed by, nor explicable in terms of, the properties of hydrogen and oxygen, must be the experience of wetness (as much a mental event as pain). If all that is meant is 'how water molecules objectively behave', that *is* explicable in terms of their constituent atoms, and not an emergent property at all. You will notice that I am here simply ignoring the long and useless detour through merely Humean causation (a topic which I shall touch upon in my third volume).

The third option, banking on some future theory that would show us either that mental events are physically intelligible (in terms of our present objectivist mythology of physics), or else that they are intelligible in terms of an as-yet-unformulated panpsychism, amounts to a draft upon the future that we have not the slightest rational expectation of being able to meet. Popular mythology notwithstanding we are not in any danger at all of finding ourselves (or our masters) equipped with an intelligibly grounded theory about the physical causes of the mental. Adrenalin may be a better metaphor than boiling blood, but at least no one ever supposed that blood 'literally' boiled, nor that its doing so explained the desire for revenge, nor that that was all that was happening 'in' the enraged person. Modernists who criticize 'occultists' for confusing metaphor and literal truth can sometimes be astonishingly credulous of the metaphors deployed by modern materialists.

Appeals to neurological evidence that mechanical or electrical stimulation of the brain immediately causes the person whose brain it is to have certain experiences are also irrelevant. The fact is that such stimulation does not cause the patient to make decisions or voluntarily to fantasize (see Penfield 1975: 77): the patient—at best—merely comments on the images that then float across her mental view, and we need no spirit come from the grave to remind us that our thoughts and fantasies are not entirely ours. On the present evidence our will is not an epiphenomenon of brain activity, and such thoughts and fantasies as are occasioned by such artificial stimuli are not the same things as the stimuli.

So we can be as confident as ever that there are some mental events additional to any physical ones that we have yet identified (that is, to any events that can be grasped as the mathematically predictable outcome of objectively discernible forces). Our pains are something extra in the world such that one who feels no pains of her own cannot understand what we are talking about however much neurology she learns.

That pains and the like should prove to be merely epiphenomenal, so that all the real causal work is done at a physical level, is an equally bizarre idea, one that conflicts with our own ready experience, and which leaves us with even less understanding of why there should be pains. If cave-fish lose the sight of their eyes because there is nothing to weed out blind or myopic fish, why have we not all lost the real presence of pain, if evolutionary selection cannot get a grip upon real pains, but only on the behaviour associated with them (see Puccetti 1975)? Perhaps we have—or maybe only physicalist philosophers are thus deprived! For the thought does occasionally cross my mind that perhaps some entities I had believed were humans, and philosophers, are indeed such empty shells as they purport to think!

But we can now return to the first objection to mere physicalism. A pain is a mental event not so much because it is (or might be thought to be) a 'private' one but because its intrinsic painfulness amounts to the victim's unavoidable dislike of it. We cannot avoid a reference to an experiencing subject (who can even, within some limits, modify her own experience) in saying what a pain is. 'It hurts' commits me to a preference that it should go away! Sheer privacy was not the point even for Descartes (whose God, after all, knew all that any of us truly know). Transparency (such that if it hurts there must be someone who experiences that hurt) is a Cartesian requirement of greater plausibility—though Cartesians too easily interpret this as a requirement that someone 'knows' it hurts. A child may not yet know (be able to work out or say) that 'hurting' is what is happening: she still hurts. But such transparency applies more widely still. It is not only things 'happening in my head' that must be given mentalistic or transparent descriptions: even my typing out these words, or saying them, are events such that, if they occur, there must be someone who knows they do, and someone whose intention is crucial in identifying just what they are. Without such intentional causality and transparency there are no such real events.

Dennett's attempt to argue, without resorting to pan-psychism, that an apple-tree's 'behaviour' can be correctly, because sometimes usefully, described with intentional cate-gories, merely evades the issue by imputing reality to metaphors without bothering to describe a metaphysic that would license the move (Dennett 1978: 272).

This is not to say that I here-now must be conscious of all those intentions that might plausibly be attributed to the being that is Me. 'I' is a term—I hope the point is, by now, an obvious one—that can be used most variously, and especially for that little wandering light of present consciousness that occasionally flares up to form a real attention. My claim is only that someone is consciously engaged in whatever can correctly be described intentionally. That someone, small mind, demon, god, or dryad, may turn out to be a segment of the waking soul, or else a spirit to be forever barred from that coming or eternal union—though my own suspicion is that it will usually be the former.

The Politics of Philosophical Psychology

So what is the relation of such mentalistic description and explanation to the 'merely physical'? Every act of mine will, so it seems, be enacted in a physically described world, and in accordance with statistical regularities that strongly suggest the presence of physical mechanisms to 'generate' those actions. Our acts, no doubt, or images of those acts, could only be physically generated by a machine of such stupendous complexity as to be utterly useless for predictive purposes. It is easier to predict the behaviour of living organisms of any moderate level of complexity simply by imagining ourselves beneath their skin than to attempt to work out the synergistic by-play of biochemical exchange which is, presumably, going on. Only when we lack a grip of what it is like to be a bat or a bumble bee, or when the ends apparently served by some small mind are ones that we cannot entertain as ours, is there any need to imagine how some simple physical model of the creature might 'behave'. And it would be fallacious to conclude even from the invariable predictive success of such a model (unattested) that there is really any topologically similar structure at work in bat or bee.

We have no detailed and accurate model of the biochemical reactions that occur even in the transformation of acorn into oak, or those that would occur if nothing else played any part in that transformation. Whereas we no longer need (or no longer think we need) to invoke spiritual rulers of the planets to model the paths they tread (since Newtonian, or Einsteinian, models give us as much detail as we need), we cannot make any similar claim about living organisms (and especially, of course, the 'higher mammals'). We do not know whether chemicals alone would mirror or mimic animal behaviour, without appeal to ghosts in the machine, because we are incapable of completing a study of their synergistic activity within any useful period. In some relatively simple cases we can give the impression that we have produced a mechanical model (though not one that reaches down to the chemical level), by discriminating a few action patterns in the organism under review. Investigators regularly conclude that there is then no need to postulate extra spiritual or intentional causes for the movements of, say, a woodlouse. But such action patterns are confessedly no more than patterns, not explanations why, and do not rival empathy as serious predictors.

We can, on the other hand, predict such behaviour in most familiar cases with a high level of success if we assume that animals do things of much the same kind as we do, even if their particular goals differ. Folk-psychology is enormously successful, and has no serious empirically grounded rival, although the insights of mind-modellers have made some contribution to the body of folk-psychological understanding. The claim dogmatically asserted by the Churchlands, that 'folk-psychology' (simple-mindedly summarized) is an unsuccessful or declining research programme (see Churchland 1984), is simply false. In cases where the animal under study—say, a hunting wasp—does not act as we would expect her to if she genuinely had, say, the welfare of her young in mind experimentalists conclude that her behaviour is mechanically determined. But we might as easily conclude that she had other goals: human beings, after all, are not generally thought irrational or mechanistic brutes merely because they do not much mind that their acts do not always have a consequence rationalistic observers might expect. People make love no less, simply because they cannot then make babies.

So why not conclude from the success of empathetic understanding that there are real and separate souls, pilots in the corporeal ship, incapable no doubt of steering courses that the waves and wind prevent, but not mere observers of the mechanically determined voyage? Maybe even the oaktree has a working dryad. The answer, obviously enough, is not that we have empirical evidence against this theory of sufficient strength to outweigh its obvious and unrivalled past success, but that investigators have a rooted dislike of the unweighable, of factors that can be discerned only empathetically and not defined by would-be objective measure.

And whence comes this dislike? There may be many reasons, including ones that ought to be considered by any honest epistemologist and some that draw their strength from the very division between sensory appearance and mathematically cognizable reality that Plato bequeathed us. Paradoxically, those who reject a dualism of 'soul and body' because they think that physicalist explanation in terms of the quantifiable leads us beyond the mere appearance of intentional and qualitative explanation, are themselves dualists, as convinced that there is a veil of illusion over true reality as any Platonist or Hindu. But one powerful and neglected explanation for modern preference of 'objective measure' rests in political philosophy. It has been important to a mobile and entrepreneurial culture that the land, the trees, the tools of trade, the high heavens, and even human bodies be emptied of their spirits—which is to say, of our empathetic engagement. The tribesmen who feel themselves to be 'part' of the land, united with their ancestors and the spirits of place and wild things, will not readily dispose of those same holy places. What they may 'sell', or give in exchange, to colonists can only be the liberty to enjoy the fruits of the land (as Thomas Jefferson himself proposed). That they live in an animated, spiritual world is, first of all, a political fact—and as I pointed out earlier, the facts of their subjective world are such as either to demand a dualism of appearance and reality or else to show that the presence of gods is not incompatible with there also being accurately quantifiable aspects of the land they live by. That their would-be masters, armed with abstract theories of individual autonomy and human right, prefer to weigh the land out, and the fruits of it, is no surprise. What is perhaps surprising is that those same moderns believe themselves to be free of ideology, and suppose that, though they have denied that anything at all is sacred, yet their own human purposes still are.

That mind-set that empties the object-world of significance and so leaves us free to manipulate it undisturbed by guardian spirits (who, no doubt, have their only natural residence 'within the mind') has been alternately praised and denounced: praised, as freeing us from religious tyranny into the 'glorious liberty of the sons of God'; denounced, as leaving nature unprotected against rape. Those Christian apologists of the 1960s who claimed 'secularism' as a triumph for the true Christian gospel were sadly upstaged by ecomystics in the 1970s, who agreed that it was the Christians who had banished the old gods and despised them for it. My own view is that the 1960s' secularists were astoundingly naïve to suppose that they could welcome the world's 'disenchantment' and somehow keep humanity intact. Though they professed to be anti-Cartesian in their zeal to do away with the split between soul and body, sacred and profane, they were in fact as Cartesian as Jacques Monod, who proclaimed himself and 'modern man' as free to choose whatever world he pleased while simultaneously decreeing that the 'real world' (which after all included us) was strictly mechanistic. Somehow the Cartesian observer and his wishes were immune to sceptical deconstruction—which is perhaps hardly surprising. On the one hand, it is strictly impossible to think that one's own thoughts mean nothing, that they are no more than mechanically contrived cerebral episodes (so that all attempts to propound this thesis are pragmatically self-refuting); on the other, the very emotional and political purpose that underlies the willed 'disenchantment' of the world, to empty the world of anything that might resist our will, precisely elevates that will as something not to be thought away.

Real Explanations

So what is the relationship between the world of quantifiable event and non-teleonomic process, and the manifold worlds of consciousness, intention, feeling? Single-subject theories usually turn out to be materialist: one identifiable thing is five and a half feet tall, weighs one hundred and forty pounds, likes raspberries and *Hill Street Blues*, believes in God and the gold standard, has an ache in her left upper arm. No doubt: but the real question is, where do we find an explanation for those properties? What properties must we impute to the first elements of reality if such a being is to exist? Ordinarily physical objects, we suppose, can rightly be decomposed—in thought—and their more usual properties identified as results of those imaginable properties imputed to the currently fashionable range of elementary particles. Those ultimate constituents may not now be imagined quite as tiny billiard balls: it may turn out that even to speak of one such particle alone in all the world is quite absurd, and that the real constituents of measurable reality are fields coterminous with the universe, never really to be understood in isolation. Some physicists, impressed by Schrodinger, have drifted toward some idealist theory, that rejects the notion of a world detached from any observer and her choices—with the odd result that neuropsychologists and biologists are busily 'reducing' human thought to a supposedly more solid base in physical reality while physicists are undermining that same physicality. What seems especially puzzling in all this is that people seem to have no difficulty in believing both that there is a world discoverable by scientific investigation that is the real cause and context of human evolution and invention, and that it is merely superstitious to suppose that how the world is could be specified at all apart from human thought. As Barfield has pointed out—only to be jeered at for his pains—this is like suggesting that the figures of the Zodiac (which are obviously no more than human constructions) should be mentioned in a properly objective account of how the human species came to be (Barfield 1965). Or as Fawcett mockingly remarked: if matter is only a 'logical construction' it ought to have better manners than to roll like Juggernaut over all human aspirations and the logic that constructed it (Fawcett 1921: 11 f.).

Cartesians and physicalists—or in an earlier metaphor, the gods and giants—continue to dispute in every human generation and every human soul. On the one hand, we can see that all we are and do is of a piece with what occurs 'outside' our thought: we can do nothing without its being the case that measurable changes do occur in ways that can in part, though often very loosely, be modelled in non-intentional mechanisms. Whatever we do humanly will also be done physically, though we cannot in fact tell whether it is always (or even ever) what 'would be done by mere mechanical contrivance' even if that mechanistic world were a closed universe. On the other hand, we cannot think away our own interpretative, choosing presence. The objects postulated by physical sciences do not now explain—and on some accounts depend upon—that subjective reality. Both descriptions are, or may be, accurate, but the question still remains: which level of description is it that points us to real explanation, or else what are the real identities at work in the world? Either the merely physical or objective description, devised to disenchant the world, is to be preferred (although it cannot in the end permit us to prefer at all and cannot give good reason to suppose that beings in such a universe could ever locate the truth of it), or the intentional, personalistic description is closer to the unimagined truth and what we model to ourselves as 'merely physical' is itself the epiphenomenon.

Perhaps you will not be surprised to hear that I prefer the second option. The presences and multiply determined choices of free spirits are mirrored in each other's consciousness: their doings are an uninterrupted babble from which they (we) excerpt such strands of conversation as we find relevant. No one can thus say anything without the partial co-operation of uncounted others, each with their own whims and fancies. It is not surprising that what I now consider 'me' does not always get its own way. Particular occasions, maybe, can be modelled (as one might allow a computer program to produce successive sentences as 'the cat sat on the mat' or 'the duck jumped on the rug' by mere substitution): as one attempts to model more and more of the created universe without reference to the creative spirits whose converse it is one has to invent yet more particles, quaint dimensions, and unexampled reverses—which is why the joke that God, having forgotten about the elementary particles when He created the world, is now making them up as He goes along, has a certain charm. I do not mean that we should not attempt such non-intentional accounts: their merit is exactly that they can be called upon when we do not know or cannot imagine what particular imagined spirits might have in mind to do. They constitute a mental discipline which, in its proper place, saves us from too quick an identification of what others want. This is so even at an obviously person-to-person level: if I am too inclined to think that women fancy me I would be well advised to try and empty my thoughts of them of sexual affect, to try and see them with a degree of 'objectivity'. But of course if I could discover what they really meant and felt that would be the better option, and I certainly should not try and secure myself against temptation by seeing them only as so much moving matter. Just so, we may be well advised to drive away the thought that lightning strikes where we would have it strike, that the thoughts of cloud-gathering Zeus are just like mine—but it does not follow from that necessary discipline that we should deny the lightning any meaning.

The elegant little worlds of physicists or physiologists, described without personal affect in obedience to some difficult idea of beauty, themselves encapsulate great myths, symbolical utterances—which is why they do so often seem to re-embody ancient stories, of how 'things fall apart, the centre cannot hold', or how our little lives crawled out from the body of a great dead giant to serve the gods of love and justice. Those worlds which materialists declare to be the real substratum of our mistaken lives (although no explanation of the link is yet forthcoming, and although there seems no way that those same worlds could be the object of any cognitive state of ours) are better conceived as models, metaphors, partial descriptions of the infinite reaches of the world of meaning. They are made, as much as any heathen idol is, and as Weil (1987: 247) remarks, 'the fetishists are superior to us'. We have deliberately constructed an 'objective world', that is to say a world perceived without reverence and interrogated by experimental techniques expressly designed to rule out the disturbing effects of any other demon than far-sighted Apollo. We have then proposed that all other ways of world-making are of so little significance as not really to exist at all. In saying this much I may seem to align myself too closely with those social idealists who take truth to be only what is affirmed by currently accepted rules, which rules of course may differ from one moment or subculture to another. But my conclusion, like Duerr's, is more radical, more Platonic than Protagorean. The atoms, fields, or elementary particles of physics, and the neutral networks of physiologists are not necessarily mere figments; and it is certainly no part of my design to forget the axiom of the Way of Truth, that there is one Truth only, even if there are many little images of it. If physicists or physiologists are on the right way it is because their models are the symbols of those 'giants who formed the world into its sensual existence and now live in it in chains'. Renaissance occultists identified, through self-reflective meditation, those forms of life and character that moved in them and in the 'outer' world. The more foolish of them, maybe, thought the metaphors they used to catch those spiritual forms had literal existences behind the veil of sense. If that was foolish, so is it also to imagine that any of our stories can describe in any literal sense what the world looked like before there were any lives around to see it, or that our minimalist analysis demands a similarly minimal ontology.

Whatever lies behind the veil of sense, we may believe, has woven its nets in subtle, mathematically described, beauty. Of that real world we may know very little, even that it does indeed have the beauty we expect in it. One thing we do know: even if we do not quite know what it is like to be a bat or dung-beetle, we do know what it is like to be us. What we are, the things that seem to have two natures, or that can be accurately described at many levels, is in the end to be explained intentionally.

8

The Controlling Daimon

Truth and Obedience

All truly modern minds are agreed that there can be no duties of obedience, nor any thing that has authority over the unconsenting agent—following in this, though without full understanding, Locke's dictum that the only source of political authority is the subject's own consent (*Second Treatise* 95 (1963: 374)). That is why, such modern minds propose, there can be no God, nor any objective obligation, binding irrespective of the subject's will. Nothing at all could be God, because nothing could have that degree of moral authority. Some of those who argue against God as a source of moral obligation imagine that there might yet be some impersonal Moral Law (and that God-fearers are condemned by that impersonal standard). More consistent moderns recognize that any such Law is just as offensive to the self-governing agent (as Perry 1976: 31 f.)—though they rarely draw the obvious conclusion that there can, in that case, be no objective wrong done in vowing perpetual obedience to anyone one pleases. Many moral philosophers nowadays are, in other words, 'of the Devil's party without knowing it':

> The mind is its own place, and in itself
> can make a Heav'n of Hell, a Hell of Heaven.
> What matter where, if I be still the same?
> Better to reign in Hell than serve in Heav'n.
>
> (Milton, *Paradise Lost* 1.254 ff.)

What is strange about this praise of individual autonomy is that moderns so often think that they are Kantian, whereas it is clear that Kant himself—like Locke—wrote in an older, and much healthier, tradition, for which the individual ego was not the sole appropriate authority even for itself, and the well-ordered soul emphatically not Satan. On the contrary, those who are led by egoistic concerns, by what Aurobindo called the 'enormous gnome' that intrudes upon the exhausting whirlwind of those thoughts we miscall ours, are most truly slaves. What is even stranger, of course, is that those moralists who proclaim the Satanic path imagine that they can somehow reconstruct something resembling traditional or bourgeois morals, and expect the rest of us to be persuaded! The moral or pseudo-moral codes devised for their own purposes by desperate ruffians are seriously offered as examples of how well and fruitfully Satanic wills can work, without any attempt to ask how such self-devised strategies have actually operated in the past. So Mackie: 'the truest teachers of moral philosophy are the outlaws and thieves who keep faith and rules of justice with one another . . . as rules of convenience without which they cannot hold together' (Mackie 1976: 10). And whoever said they did?

In place of amoralism and the disobedient will, I wish to offer that other, and older, image of the controlling *daimon*: *nous*, conscience, or the word of God. In accordance with the overall strategy of this volume, I am speaking phenomenologically or psychologically, about life as we experience it. But I can hardly avoid, as I have hardly avoided in past chapters, giving hints about cosmology. After all, the very thing I was drawing to your attention in the last chapter was the extent to which we do have an interior knowledge of the way things are. When we understand ourselves, we understand the world, and we come to do the former by considering what it is to understand.

One perennial answer to sceptical doubts about the foundations of morality and ordinary belief is the insistence that 'ordinary moral and practical discourse' cannot thus be called into question, that it constitutes the ineliminable framework of all we do and think. It is my conviction that this response is in fact indistinguishable from that made by the ancient sceptics, a willed submission to the quadruple compulsion of nature, sensation, custom, and the rules of such crafts as we elect to practise 'so as not to be wholly inactive' (Sextus, *Outlines* 1. 11; see Hume (1. 4. 7) 1888: 269). Those philosophers who offer this supposed solution also, so it seems to me, gravely underestimate the complexity and openness of

common discourse. What they propose as the one, unquest-
ionable framework for moral and metaphysical 'knowledge'
usually turns out to be their own simplified version of the
beliefs and practices taken most seriously by members of their
own clique, or club, or college. When they claim that moral
and metaphysical 'hypotheses' are 'true' simply if enough of
'us' say they are, they commonly forget what people have said
in the past, and what many of them still say. The new
conventionalism would never have allowed honest rationalists
to question the existence of witches, spirits, and moral
pollution, but now forbids us even to consider the existence of
such things on no better ground than that the conventionalists' friends and family do not like us to.

> Too many philosophers . . . appeal to our ordinary ways of talking
> about 'language', 'conventions', 'intentions' and so on as if they
> could thus browbeat us into believing that we don't talk seriously
> when we talk in ways they find philosophically distasteful—as if this
> were obvious! (King-Farlow 1978: 41)

How moral or political individualism can survive the on-
slaught of the new conventionalism I do not know. Even if
there were good arguments for the 'real truth' of conventionalism (and if there were, of course, that would be enough to
refute conventionalism!), there are good pragmatic reasons to
prefer a non-dogmatic realism. Instead of relying (usually
without any empirical evidence) on the conventionalist's
personal opinion as to what 'the conventions' actually are,
and her assertion that 'we cannot question' what philosophers
throughout history have in fact questioned, let us seek to draw
up presently unconventional answers, to exorcize the idols of
the theatre and tribe. Popular answers to our moral and
metaphysical problems are, popularly, meant as answers, not
as moves in a power-struggle (it is odd that few philosophical
conventionalists take much account of the obvious moral of
their thesis, that rational and philosophical debate can only be
propaganda for their own class-interest . . .). Popular, semi-
popular, and unpopular answers may be true or false, even if
we sometimes have little hope of settling the question. We
have no hope at all if we are not prepared to analyse and
develop answers different from the ones we are 'authorit-

atively' told are popular. 'The commonest sense is the sense of men asleep, which they express by snoring' (Thoreau 1910: 286).[1]

What can we learn about presently popular doctrines by directing our attention to presently unpopular or unimagined alternatives? Without such a deliberate refocusing, it seems to me, we may well forget even the real merits of 'our own' synthesis, and the real point even of questions that we have allowed a place in philosophical discourse. One example of this that I shall address at greater length in the next volume is the problem of the Cartesian demon (or its modern avatar, the mad neurological surgeon): no one who studied this question in an undergraduate course would be likely to have had it drawn to her attention that anyone has ever seriously believed that this life was indeed 'a dream and a delusion' (Aurelius, *Meditations* 2. 17. 1), and that this made a genuine difference to their life. But of course many people have believed exactly that, and not to realize this is simply not to understand what is at issue.

Similarly—and now at last I approach the central topic of this chapter—when we read that what matters more than anything else in us is *nous*, and that this *nous* is a *daimon*, no real part of the psycho-physical organism we call a human animal, there is a tendency to insist, first, that no one goal or value can be so dominant, and second, that to make such a division between *nous* and the Soul (which is to say, the mental capacities of a certain sort of social animal) is an ill-digested relic of Platonic or Cartesian dualism—and therefore obviously false. Modernist commentators rarely notice that they are rejecting an ancient and world-wide tradition, namely that there is an Unborn and Indestructible which is worth more than anything else, which is an intruder upon the bourgeois certainties of the market-place and assembly but which is also our truest and deepest Self. At the same time commentators hardly seem to notice what the consequence of rejecting this tradition is. According to Sankara:

[1] An earlier version of this chapter was tried out on a conference on Ancient and Modern Concepts of the Person, now anthologized as Clark 1990. I am grateful especially to Christopher Gill, Mary Midgley, and T. Engberg-Pedersen for their comments.

Since the Self is the witness of the body, its acts, its states, therefore the Self must be of other nature than the body . . . Of this compound of skin, flesh, fat, bone and water, the man of deluded mind thinks, 'This is I'; but he who is possessed of judgement knows that his true Self is of other character, in nature transcendental. (Head and Cranston 1977: 56 ff.)

The modernist neither agrees that the Self is something other than the physical and emotional being with which we normally identify ourselves, nor that she is no more than a compound of skin, flesh, fat, and bone. The 'human rights' that liberals value are not obviously at home in a godless universe, where human animals are not distinctively different from the beasts that perish, and what are now, conventionally, called 'my' body and property, 'my' past or future, 'my' achievements and ideas are 'mine' only by current linguistic agreement (and might as accurately be someone else's). Nor can we easily distinguish between a life (which may be more or less rich, worthwhile, and satisfying) and the one who lives that life (whom good liberals do not wish to think less 'intrinsically valuable' than any other) without an anti-empiricist insistence on real identities. It is apparently assumed—without good argument—that no matter what we turn out to be (or assume ourselves to be) we can reasonably maintain exactly the same moral and political code (suitably and quietly amended by class-interest) that once went with quite a different view of what and where we were. Those commentators who notice the problem make some vague gesture towards G. E. Moore's discussion of the 'naturalistic fallacy', as if this excused them from any further examination of the moral and practical implications of modernism. But Gautama was correct:

There is an Unborn, Unoriginated, Uncreated, Unformed. If there were not this Unborn, this Unoriginated, this Uncreated, this Unformed, escape from the world of the born, the originated, the created, the formed would be impossible. (Goddard 1970: 32)

And in that case we should have no good ground for supposing that human reason was anything but 'a little agitation of the brain', a motion wholly incapable of serving as a model for the world at large. It is because *nous* is more than

an agitation of the brain that we can hope to strip off the soul's
tunic of opinion and imagery to enter the Holy of Holies
(Philo, *LA* 2. 56; see Dodds 1968: 95), and begin to
understand the world we really inhabit. 'This is what we
mean by possession of spirit: to be involved with everything
that exists, "to permeate the whole cosmos" ' (Pieper 1965:
75). If that is not possible, or not to be expected, then perhaps
the Sceptics have the victory after all—but if they do, then the
whole house of cards that modernists have erected against the
claims of the perennial philosophy comes tumbling down.

Reason as Daimon

What then do I mean by speaking of Reason as 'the
Controlling *Daimon*'? One possible interpretation, worth
mentioning to convey a warning, is that the rules and
techniques of reason be regarded as demonic, such as may at
last disrupt a decent and humane existence. Demons, popularly
so-called, are intrusive elementals, at war with Heaven and
with humankind's true self. Their powers are real, but must
be put at the service of humane endeavour. Ares and
Aphrodite, great Olympians, are still readily conceived as
powers that can shake the human heart and world. Aphrodite
Ouranios, despite Plato's joking transvaluation of values
(*Symposium* 180 D), is a Titan, an untamed power that owes no
duty to the God of Justice and Hospitality: before she becomes
Olympian, deserving of her own due honour, she must be
born of Zeus and Dione. Metis, who is crafty wisdom, must
also be swallowed up by Zeus and reborn as Athene (Detienne
and Vernant 1978: 108 f.). Reason as cleverness or intellectual
technique, and reason as the objectifying eye of far-shooting
Apollo, must be put to service lest they destroy humane order.
Intellectual curiosity, as I have emphasized before, has no
more title than any other overmastering passion to our whole
devotion. The thought is indeed the truth behind the
commentators' casual rejection of the thought that some one
thing, like *nous*, could count for more than anything else. If
cleverness or science were such a value then nothing could be

wrong that was clever or scientific: but we know very well that only barbarians think that 'science' excuses all, or that a clever piece of work is its own justification.

The techniques and rules of practical and theoretical reason may be intrusive, domineering, and destructive (quite as much as homicidal fury, intoxication, or sexual desire): in brief, they may be considered demonic, even by those who have no serious ontological commitment to the separate existence of demons. 'I define "daimonic" as any natural function in the individual that has the power of taking over the whole person. Sex and eros, anger and rage and the craving for power are examples' (May 1970: 196). Demons, or the demonic, are real and powerful elements in human character, and the less we think that there is some one thing, the Self, in each of us the less we can claim that 'reason' or the operations of reason have any different status from lust or anger or the rules of etiquette. If there were a real Self, and 'Reason' were another name for it, then 'Reason' names no *daimon* in the sense of something that might disrupt the whole system of the individual personality or of society. Other moods or modes of human existence might prove disruptive, but 'reason' named the still centre of the individual soul, the point where all souls might agree. Without that conviction, 'Reason' names only a set of animal capacities as little to be trusted as any other.

This is part of what it might mean to speak of 'reason as *daimon*', but it is not my central theme. The *daimon* that *nous* or Reason is is not wholly and straightforwardly to be identified with the Ego-consciousness, but neither is it an intrusive and destructive element that must be made to serve some yet higher value in the personality or in society lest it prove demon. If the life well-lived is *eudaimonia*, 'having a good *daimon*', and that *daimon* is *nous*, as Xenocrates (fr. 81; see Aristotle, *Topics* 2, 112^a 32) suggested, it is not surprising that to be *eudaimon* we must identify ourselves with *nous*, with what is most especially ourselves and yet something more than human (Aristotle, *Nicomachean Ethics* 10, 1177^b 26 ff.). *Nous* is (*a*)the most valuable and god-like element of the human organism, (*b*) the organ of fundamental intellectual intuition, of those truths that cannot without absurdity be supposed to be demonstrated from yet firmer truths, (*c*) conscience or consciousness itself (though this last perhaps goes beyond what earlier Hellenic thinkers would have said).

It may be true, as Aristotle said, that there are many things we value for themselves, irrespective of any further good they do. It is also true, as Aristotle also said, that there are some things which, when we have to choose, we certainly should prefer. Those who wish to live a life well-lived will recognize many duties that, as occasions offer, they must fulfil: that is the truth hidden in the claim that most modern commentators make, that *eudaimonia* must be taken to be an 'inclusive' concept, incorporating everything that the person of sound judgement does or should prefer. But it cannot be thought that the fulfilling of those duties is, in the abstract, what the person of sound judgement would choose to be doing. If it were possible we would choose to have no occasion to act bravely, temperately, justly, or the rest. Action in accordance with moral virtue is predicated on needs and misfortunes that we would not wish for. If we seriously thought that the exercise of courage or compassion was the highest good, we should be compelled to create occasions for such exercise if none were forthcoming in the course of nature: good Samaritans need people who have been mugged. Those imaginable or real beings who have escaped such occasions do not live less well than we do, so long as they exercise the higher, independent virtues, and are—correspondingly— possessed of the sort of character that would, if it were necessary, be expressed in moral action.

So what is it that each of us would wish to be and see? What would it be that we would never surrender? Aristotle's answer was that it would be the life lived according to the best and highest virtue, even though that life is more than humankind can hope for, in these or any other troubled times. That virtue is one that needs no occasion for its proper exercise, nor any equipment beyond the immediate power of the agent. Contemplative virtue is an excellence that allows us to stand a little apart from our ordinary selves: 'I am conscious of the presence and criticism of a part of me which, as it were, is not a part of me, but a spectator, sharing no experience but taking note of it, and that is no more I than it is you' (Thoreau 1910: 119). Thoreau's account makes clear, what Aristotle unfortunately does not, that the part or non-part of me which is spectator can also stand in judgement over my own moral action. It is because I can see the whole of which this organism here is a part that I can pretend to a more objective, morally critical stance. If I could not thus stand over against myself I should be limited (of course without knowing it) by my immediate desires and prejudices. What contemplates in me is conscience. As Jerome declared, *synteresis* is a fourth element of the soul, symbolized by the eagle of Ezekiel's vision, 'which is not mixed up with the other three but corrects them when they go wrong, and of which we read in the scriptures as the spirit which intercedes for us with ineffable groaning' (Jerome in Ezekiel 1: 7: Potts 1980: 6 f.). Potts, revealingly enough, does not pick up Jerome's clear statement that the eagle is separate, not straightforwardly a part of the whole human creature, but relapses on the modern convention that conscience is simply one faculty of the soul.

Separation, distance, is a phenomenon. If one is threatened or beguiled for a moment longer than would have sealed one's fate, if one is not caught napping, then one may suddenly feel the web of control dissolve. Suddenly the threats or bribes mean nothing: one is stepped aside, released, an onlooker who may then choose to act. True choice arises only from that distanced, balanced look. We may not relish its arrival (for it is a frightening enough thought that in a moment we shall not be frightened of what now frightens us, and dispiriting enough to think that we shall suddenly not want what now seems most desirable!), and we may even choose to throw ourselves back into involvement in the bodily and social nexus, forgetting that momentary gleam. More terribly still we may grow proud of our new, godlike insight, and so transform it into one more egoistic conceit. It is as well to retain the ancient insight, that in these moments of noetic insight we are allowed a glimpse through eyes that are not quite our own. Conscience, as our predecessors thought, was in essence the voice of a wider and greater spirit than our common self, a critical commentator which was citizen of a greater kingdom. Heracleitos' obscure comment that '*ethos anthropoi daimon*' (22 B 119 DK) quite likely makes a similar point: not that it is a person's character which determines his fortune ('the fault, dear Brutus, lies not in our stars, but in ourselves') (Vernant and Vidal-Naquet 1981: 13). Socrates' *daimon*, as it was understood by later commentators, operates as Philo of Alexandria reckoned conscience did, not as a force innate in and the property of the human soul. Yeats' description of 'the voice of conscience': 'It is a voice in my head that is sudden and startling. It does not tell me what to do but often reproves me. It will say perhaps "That is unjust" of some thought; and once when I complained that a prayer had not been heard, it said, "You have been helped" '. One critic comments: 'It is not an almost exact description of Socrates' *daimon*?' Actually, it is not, and only a minority of later commentators deliberately and openly equated *nous*, conscience and guardian *daimon* (as Plutarch, *De Facie* 943ᵃ), probably because not everyone is actually led by *nous*, but those who did seem to have caught hold of a significant point. Plato's picture of the whole psychic organism, especially in the *Timaeus*, is of a divinely created *nous*, encapsulated and barnacled (*Republic* 10, 612 A) by other psychic functions with which it is not identical.

It would be too easy just to say that for Plato, a divine spirit given to man by God was indwelling in man too, and that man's most proper life-task was honouring and cultivating that divine spirit that dwells within himself. Yet it should be noted that this was literally what Plato said. (De Vogel 1981: 2)

I would add that this is 'too easy' only in the sense that we run the risk of ignoring genuine puzzles when we compare great metaphysical systems. It does not seem to me to be false to Plato's intention.

The awakening in us of this wider vision of things, and a correspondingly critical attitude to the ordinary self, can be prompted by ethical or by aesthetic factors. 'Beauty can prod man out of the realm of comprehensible habituation, out of the "interpreted world" ' (Pieper 1965: 81). Beauty, in the radical sense that we often prefer to ignore, is a reminder that things are not tools or ornaments for our everyday purposes, not even objects of our comfortable aestheticism. True beauty may be 'terrible as an army with banners', a power that makes demands and sets up ever higher standards. The love awakened by such beauty may be contaminated by concupiscence and personal fear, but it points toward its own purification, to the demand that the beautiful simply be, even if the lover, as single, temporal creature never yet enjoy it (see Pieper 1969:20 f.). 'Love is important only in Plato's sense, in so far as it gives wings to the imagination—whatever in love is personal and not imaginative, matters not at all' (Raine 1956: xiv). The awakening may also come, remember, with the discovery of our own ordinary self's mortality. It is because we can be aware of a wider world in which this self has ceased to be that we can contemplate our death, and in the contemplating of it know ourselves—our higher self—to be immortal. 'That which experiences and knows about the divine and consequently about the universe is identical with his own being . . . the divine is man's own being' (Verdenius 1942: 29).

The objective, critical mind that wakens in us enables us to see before and after our ordinary self's life. 'Memory'—by which is meant the impersonal memory of science and tradition—'is exalted because it is the power that makes it possible for men to escape time and return to the divine state' (Vernant 1983: 88). 'The effort involved in remembering makes it possible for us to learn who we are and to know our own psyche—that *daimon* which has become incarnate in us' (Vernant 1983: 86). If the world before 'my' birth and after 'my' death is present to me, the Self it is present to is something more than the complex of desires and personal memories that moderns now equate with my 'real' or 'true' self. The Self of which the ancients, in Greece, India, and elsewhere, were speaking is something of which we catch a glimpse in these various experiences and activities. That Self, which we dignify by the title of Conscience, Consciousness, Mind, is what no one who has experienced its presence would give up, and which is the condition of moral action in the world where we find ourselves. Those who set themselves to live from that standard make discoveries:

The more the seeker learns to listen above, to follow the intimations of the Silence (which are not imperious, not noisy, which are almost imperceptible like a breath, hardly thought out, only felt, but terribly rapid), the more numerous, exact, irresistible they become; and gradually he sees that all his acts, the very least, can be sovereignly guided by this silent source above, that all his thoughts come from there, luminous, beyond dispute, that a sort of spontaneous knowledge is born in him. (Satprem 1968: 190).

I add in passing that the strange remark of the Pythagoreans, that myriads of souls can be seen dancing in a sunbeam (Aristotle, *De Anima* 1, 404^a 17 ff.), is matched by the report from Aurobindo's ashram that supramental illumination is 'like a vivid gold, a warm gold dust . . . a crowd of tiny little points of light, nothing but that'. One frequent conclusion is, unsurprisingly, that this Self whose knowledge reaches out to embrace the whole world and which far transcends our own individualities, is numerically the same in each of us. 'To be possessed of spirit is to be involved with everything that exists, to permeate the whole cosmos' (Pieper 1965: 75). That awakening centre—or rather, since it is not possible that it should ever be anything but awake—that centre as we awaken to it, is described, after Aurobindo, as follows:

Not only an impersonal force but a presence, a being in our depths, as though we had a support there, something that gives us a solidity, almost a backbone, and a quiet outlook on the world. With this little vibrating thing within, one is invulnerable and no longer alone. It is there everywhere, it is there always. It is warm, close, strong. And strangely enough when one has discovered it it is the same thing everywhere in all beings, all things the fundamental reality of our being, ourself, truly ourself, the active centre, warmth and being, consciousness and force. (Satprem 1968: 61).

Identity and Atman

It is, of course, open to us to agree with the modern psychologist that '[while] an adult person may find himself toying with the idea of having an acute personal difficulty eliminated by magical appeal to some imaginary guardian angel, [it is a mark of hysterical dissociation that it is] devoid of the actor's playful as-if approach to his stage assignments' (Klein 1951: 300). Mistaking metaphors for literal truths is a mark of schizophrenic minds—and moderns! Maybe it is really obvious that nothing that is done or experienced in the human world is more than an operation of the psychophysical organisms, the social mammals that we often understand ourselves to be. Certainly the sort of consciousness I have been describing is a capacity of the human organism: we can have those experiences, can engage in those self-critical analyses, can take a wider survey of our situation. We can even go on to try and isolate what it is about our specific animal inheritance that gives us those capacities. Why is that not all there is to it? Why distinguish *Nous logizomenos* and *Nous logizesthai parekhon* (Plotinus, *Ennead* 5. 1. 10, 13 f.; see Merlan 1963: 6), the former being eternal and transcendent?

What we experience here is a consciousness whose objects range far beyond our own mortal identities, which is at once the thing most essential to our futures and puzzlingly non-identical with the appetitive and sensuous mammals that it knows us to be. We experience it also in the thought of what it would be like to be someone else: most ethical systems require us at some point to conceive how we would wish to be treated if we were a child, an immigrant, a neighbour, an animal. But this psychophysical organism here, the one called Stephen, simply could not be and never could have been James, Nazreen, Timothy, or Tabitha. In many cases Stephen could not even be supposed to be in the 'same' situation, although it is clearly imaginable that I be so. The I that could be or could have been Nazreen is not identical with Stephen (any more than it would then be identical with Nazreen). The relation between Stephen and I is not one of identity, but participation. Stephen could exist, but not be I; I could exist and not be Stephen. Accordingly 'Stephen' and 'I' do not, for moral purposes, name the same thing (see Vendler 1985; Madell 1981: 26, 78 ff.). The I, the Self that awakens in Stephen (or rather, that Stephen occasionally wakes up to share) is the very thing that Nazreen may also 'be'.

What looks forth from another's eyes, what feels itself in the writhing of a worm, what perhaps throbs with felt if dim emotion within an electron is really the very thing which when speaking through my lips, calls itself 'I'. (Schrodinger, cited by Sprigge 1983: 274)

Just as I and Stephen can be distinguished, so must Stephen's animal capacity to be illumined be distinguished from the undying light. *Nous poietikos*, as Aristotle told us, albeit elliptically, always thinks, is unmixed and unaffected (Aristotle, *De Anima* 3, 430ᵃ 18 ff.): *Nous pathetikos* is the human animal's capacity to be enlightened, to come awake to the world that exists before and after. 'Our metaphysical centre is always conscious, but we, as sensitive-imaginative-dianoetic creatures, are not always conscious' (Warren 1964: 85). That our separate visions do not always quite agree is evidence only of our incapacity: there is still one world only which these animal intelligences reach towards, and in the end only one undying intellect (though there are many levels of consciousness between 'us' and It).

Nous comes from outside the animal (Aristotle, *De Generatione Animalium* 736ᵇ 27), and its exercise is not a bodily function even if the bodily being that receives it must have some natural capacity to receive it. 'There is no place in the cerebral cortex where electrical stimulation will cause a patient to believe or to decide . . . To suppose that consciousness or the mind has localization is a failure to understand neurophysiology' (Penfield 1975: 77). Aristotle was right to say that *nous*, consciousness strictly so called, has no bodily organ (*De Anima* 3, 429ᵇ 5), and that it is not to be explained as the product of brain, heart, or sense-organs.

But this still leaves us with the ontological problem. Granted that there are certain experiences which are recognizably alike all over the world, and in a variety of traditions; granted that there are some good reasons to take the apparent implications of those experiences seriously; granted that we cannot insist upon the unity of the ordinary self, and cannot explain at any theoretical level why creatures like us should have these experiences and capacities: what is the Self that is the invading *nous*, and what are 'we' if not that Self? To these equations Plotinus attempted answers. My exposition of those answers is very much that of an amateur where Plotinian scholarship is concerned: my only excuse is that I think I partly recognize what he is talking about, and why, although I cannot give a full exposition and justification of his psychological system within the confines of this volume.

Nous, it must be obvious by now, is not the ratiocinative or calculative faculty (*Ennead* 5. 3. 3, 15 f.):

One must not suppose that the gods or the exceedingly blessed spectators in the higher world contemplate propositions, but all the Forms we speak about are beautiful images in that world, of the kind which someone imagined to exist in the soul of the wise man, images not painted but real. (*Ennead* 5. 8. 5 20 f.)

Nor are 'we', straightforwardly, *nous*; rather is *nous* our king (*Ennead* 5. 3. 3, 32 f.): but 'we too are kings when we are in accord with it' (*Ennead* 5. 3. 4,1 f.). 'The nobly good man is the man who acts by his better part . . . *Nous* is active in the good man. He is then himself a *daimon* or on the level of *daimon* and his *daimon* is a god' (3. 4. 6, 1 ff.; see Porphyry, *Vita Plotini* 10. 15 ff.). In brief, by obeying *nous*, living in accord with that divinity, we are identified with it—and correspondingly look upward to yet higher beings. 'Every man is double, one of him is a sort of compound being and one of him is himself' (2. 3. 9, 31 f.).

He himself is the god who came Thence and his own real nature if he becomes what he was when he came, is There. When he came here he took up his dwelling with someone else whom he will make like himself to the best of the powers of his real nature, so that if possible this someone will be free from disturbance or will do nothing of which his master does not approve. (1. 2. 6, 7 ff.)

Before coming-to-be we were other men, pure souls and *nous* joined to all being (4. 4. 12). Now 'we' are in the middle: lying between *nous* and sense and able to rise or sink (5. 3. 3. 34 f.).

[The one above] knows himself according to intellect because he has become that intellect; and by that intellect he thinks himself again, not any longer as a man, but having become altogether other and snatching himself up into that higher world. (5. 3. 4, 8).

The real eternal *nous* does not come to itself from outside (5. 8. 3, 10), because it does not need to be actualized: it is itself the actuality, the presence that is multiply refracted here below. It seems likely that Plotinus intended that each partially awakened soul, binding itself to *nous*, awoke as one distinct being in a community of *noes*, which were in turn united in obedience to a god (very much as Plato's Phaedrus myth would have it). The effort to expound these twists and turns often leaves it unclear just what 'we' refers to on any particular occasion, and how many of 'us' there are meant to be. That is perhaps implicit in this whole attempt to isolate what most matters in our identities—but once again, the very question 'how many?' betrays a misunderstanding of our situation. 'The impulse to pray', said James, 'is a necessary consequence of the fact that whilst the innermost of the empirical Selves of a man is a Self of the social sort, it yet can find its only adequate Socius in an ideal world' (James 1890: i. 316).

The moments when conscience awakes in us, when we suddenly stand free of threat and bribery and the webs laid on us by others, are also, it seems to me, the moments when we are most aware of others' being. In realizing 'my own' non-identity with bodily desire and social expectation I also realize theirs. It is then that we may glimpse the possibility of a transparent, unimpeded communication. Most of the time we hear things wrongly, and cannot explain ourselves or others without introducing new errors of transmission. It is naïve to suppose that we have much experience of lucid communication: it is indeed that naïvety of naïve realism that Collingwood identified with human stupidity! But it is hardly better to decree that lucidity can never come, that we are all tied down within 'our own' subjectivities. 'Each man is different and has his own world, his own kingdom, his own reality. It is impossible to communicate the reality through another into another reality': ardent followers of Derrida should perhaps be disturbed that this is an utterance of Charles Manson (Sanders 1971: 105), an utterance with much the same content as his other claim, to have realized his own, and everyone's identity with the One (on the dangers of which see Zaehner 1974). Naïve realists have committed many crimes, but so have practising solipsists (as Wittgenstein realized, they are the very same people).

Jung's recollections of his childhood include the thought that he was, as it were, two persons: the ordinary self and its predilections, and 'the other in me was the timeless imperishable stone' (Jung 1967: 59). The thought he recorded or read back into his past is also the shaman's, who meditates on his enduring skeleton, image of what lies underneath 'the bits of flesh and fluids', anger, fear, desire, and ignorance. Plotinus'

worries about the 'boundaries of the self' (Dodds 1968: 77)
reflect a similar experience or discovery. The occult self that
Empedocles (fr. 9–12) called *daimon* and Plato identified with
the undying intellect (Dodds 1951: 43 f.),and the personal
masks with which we greet our ordinary world can both be
spoken of with the aid of personal pronouns. Our fragmentary, empirical selves are what comes to light as the undying
light plays over these fragments of existence: as the fragments
turn to the light, 'the man driven by his *daimon* steps beyond
the limits of the intermediary stage, enters the untrodden,
untreadable regions' (Jung 1967: 377).

'Abiding among the senses is a person who consists of
understanding, a light within the heart', as I have said before.
'Spirit is by nature the capacity to apprehend a world' (Pieper
1965: 92)—a world that is more than an *Umwelt*, the normal,
homely, sensed environment of a particular animal kind. To
those embedded—so far as human beings can be embedded—
in a particular, received reality, one driven by the spirit may
seem, or be, as one possessed by devils. But the spirit is
vindicated in the uncovering of a larger world. The
Upanishadic Person is at once the Self, the true subject, and
not what we in our ordinary inattention are. That undying
Self is not the moral person which moderns recognize as the
only subject. As Aquinas declared long before Strawson, the
human person is both body and soul (Pieper 1969: 40), both
signifier and embodied sign, and if this person here is to be
thought immortal it must be as a bodily being. The fault of
moderns is that we have, unaccountably, forgotten the
undying Self without ever quite admitting to ourselves what it
is really like to live in a world without it. It is perhaps worth
recalling the error of an earlier generation. Fichte's perora-
tion:

What is called death cannot interrupt my work . . . I have seized
hold upon eternity. I lift my head boldly to the threatening
precipice, to the raging cataract and to the rumbling clouds
swimming in a sea of fire, and say: I am eternal and defy your
power. Rend apart the last mote of the body I call mine: my will
alone will soar boldly and coldly above the ruins of the universe.
(Cited by Pieper 1969: 111)

But the undying intellect which is the true subject of

consciousness and conscience, the thing united in loving contemplation with all objects of all thought, is not Fichte, and does not defy the material universe. This sort of 'idealistic absolutizing of autonomous man', whether couched in Fichte's terms or in the still sillier versions of modern materialists, deserves to be countered by the blunt reminder that Socrates and Plotinus, Fichte and Nietzsche are all dead, even if—while they yet lived—the undying intellect enjoyed their service. The Will that Fichte identified with the undying Self would, to Plotinus—or so I suspect—be that mistaken desire that creates us as uncivil creatures. That is not the immortal one. Nor is romantic disaffection the same as being rooted in the eternal—a warning all too necessary in an age when 'minute philosophers' imagine that true knowledge can be found by disowning tradition and the common mind without at the same time stepping out into Jung's untrodden paths under the guidance of Another.

The Final Consolations of Philosophy

The Lady Philosophy reminded Boethius, in his death-cell, that true philosophers must think body, rank, and estate of less importance than their understanding of what was truly their own, and what permitted them. Those ancients who, not being Socrates, still thought they ought to want to be Socrates (Epictetus, *Encheiridion* 51. 3), thought of the Hebrews as a nation of philosophers, not because they asked questions, or practised a careful casuistry, but because they served God, because they saw the universe, as did Plutarch (*De Tranquillita Animi* 20), as 'a most sacred temple, into which Man is initiated by being born into it, and by becoming an awed spectator of this resplendent reality'. That common sense neglects our real setting is confirmation of Thoreau's dictum.

Beside [the schoolboy's] world there existed another realm, like a temple in which anyone who entered was transformed and suddenly overpowered by a vision of the whole cosmos, so that he could only marvel and admire, forgetful of himself. Here lived the Other, who knew God as a hidden, personal and at the same time suprapersonal secret. (Jung 1967: 61 ff.)

If moderns discuss the thought that our present life is a dream it is as a problem in epistemology, to be neutralized—like other great problems—by suggesting that it is somehow impossible to question the fundamental framework within which, they say, we live. A better understanding of that thought is as an ethical one: are we right to assume that things are as they appear to us, under the influence of desire or fear or self-esteem? The ancient answer, still worth considering, is that they are not, that this life is 'a dream and a delirium' (Aurelius 2. 17. 1), that we do not see things straight until we see with the eyes of Reason.

The supposed moral dangers of thinking this life but a dream are not so great: Epictetus believed that we began to wake precisely through our recognition of moral duty. The thought was not intended to deaden but to increase our moral seriousness. If the real world is not very much what the 'true philosophers' thought, we have no good ground to think that wisdom is worth pursuing, or even attainable. If we take philosophy—or science in general—with proper seriousness, we must try to wake up, and remember who and what we are, and what is ours. Remembering that, we can begin to glimpse, 'as through a narrow crack' (*Consolatio* 3. 9. 8), what the Lady Philosophy intended.

And what is this thing called 'I' that must not be identified with worldly wishes, wealth, bodily health, or reputation? The more softly a captive lion lives the more slavishly he lives: Epictetus imagines how a captive bird might speak: 'my nature is to fly where I please, to live in the open air, to sing when I please. You rob me of all this and then ask what is wrong with me?' (*Discourses* 4. 1. 24) Vine and cock alike do ill when they go against their nature: so also man, whose nature is not to bite, kick, imprison, or behead but to do good, to work together, to pray for the success of others (*Discourses* 4. 1. 121). The captive lion and the wicked man alike are not living the lives for which they were made, the lives which it is their nature to strive to maintain (*Consolatio* 3. 11. 49). 'There is nothing which while remaining true to its nature would try to go against God' (*Consolatio* 3. 12. 56), but it is unfortunately obvious that we often will things in opposition to the will of God, and so, allegedly, against our nature. What actually happens, of course, must under some description be what the omnipotent intends (and therefore not evil), but our intent is bad.

In an Aristotelian world, one's nature is simply what one's kind of thing characteristically and usually does unless obviously forced not to. In the absence of external pressure it seems strange to claim that what we generally do is to deny our nature. What we are, by nature, is not what now appears: '(we) have a little forgotten (our) real self', being clouded by a mist of mortal affairs that the Lady Philosophy shall wipe away (see *Consolatio* 1. 2. 13). Because our nature is to be aware of what we can be, we can conceive the negation of that self-awareness, and forget. In a Platonic world, one's nature is not what now one usually does, but what the eye of reason can discover one should do, if not perverted from the old straight way. We are, the story goes, like tiger cubs brought up by mountain goats (Zimmer 1967: 5 ff.), or like sleepers in a dream.

We are asleep as long as we are deceived, self-contradictory, inane, but Nature—which is to say, God's will—will often prod us half-awake 'though we groan and are reluctant' (*Discourses* 2. 20. 15). The more psychoanalytically inclined commentators attribute even the readiness to consider such a theme to a deep-seated malaise, a failure of nerve in the face of worldly danger. 'If only Marcus Aurelius had seen a good psychiatrist . . .' Well, what evidence is there that psychiatrists, any more than sophists, 'have the ability to impart' what they do not possess themselves, a real equanimity, and knowledge of what is really ours and what is required of us?

To be 'asleep and dreaming' is to be embedded in one's own particularity, blind to the real world which is the ground of our experience, responding to *Umwelt*-objects rather than to reals. 'For those who've woken up there is one common world; each sleeper's turned aside to a private one' (Heracleitos 22 B 89 DK). As we believe that we are awake we conclude that all those who do not notice or care about *our* objects are dreaming. We assume that people are more awake and alert the more they see things the way we 'naturally' do. But it is open to us to consider (as above) that we are as distant from a direct acquaintance with reals as we imagine them to be. The scientific world-view rests crucially on the notion that we can, through the exercise of intellectual discipline, form a notion of the real world, which then serves to reveal our ordinary visions as dreamlike. 'The act of philosophizing means that he transcends his environment and steps forth into the world' (Pieper 1952: 127). This is only believable, as I have pointed out before (Clark 1984), if we have a 'high' doctrine of reason, a very traditional belief that Reason unites us with the Powers that Be. If we believe instead that our reasoning powers, like our perceptions, are only those to be expected of placental mammals in a world governed only by Time and Chance, then we can have no rational assurance that our most carefully experimental science has any more than local, pragmatic value. Science, on those terms, no more tells us how things are, than ordinary perception does. If scientific reason gives us any access to the noumenal reality 'beyond' or 'beneath' our *Umwelten* it can only be because that reality is not quite what scientism supposes.

So far: to be asleep and dreaming is to have present to one objects not strictly identical with the causes of our being; to be turned aside into our individual or species-worlds; dream-worlds are also typified by absurdity, of logic and of value. It is a mark of what we see in dream that it does not live up to our rational demand for logical consistency: neither does the realm we fondly call waking reality: witness standard para-doxes *re* change, time, and space. These are normally 'solved ambulando'—which is to say, not solved at all, but con-sciously ignored. But there is more to the conviction that we are dreaming than logical puzzlement, just as the claim is not relevant solely to epistemology. We may also understand our ordinary goals as quite absurd—at best, quaint copies of a greater excellence: children building sand-castles to be washed away (Gregory of Nyssa, PG 44: Dodds 1968: 11).

The realities we see are like shadows of all that is God. The reality we see is as unreal compared to the reality in God as a coloured photograph compared with what it represents. . . . This whole world is made of shadows. (Cardenal 1974: 83, 99).

We are asleep because we have false impressions, false values. It is perhaps inevitable that we should: mankind cannot bear very much reality. William James cites Madame Ackerman: 'My last word will be "I have been dreaming": but in that moment she will at last have ceased to dream.'[2]

> You have forgotten what you are. Because you are wandering, forgetful of your real self, you grieve that you are an exile and stripped of your goods. Since indeed you do not know the goal and end of all things, you think that evil and wicked men are fortunate and powerful; since indeed you have forgotten what sort of governance the world is guided by, you think these fluctuations of fortune uncontrolled. (*Consolatio* 1. 6. 40).

The Fall into our present sense-world, which created things as we now see them at the same moment that it created the egos that seem to see, was the product of '*tolma*': the wish to control something as one's own (*Ennead* 4. 7, 13 etc.: Dodds 1968: 25), even if only an apple!

Jung remarks, after his near-death experiences, 'I have never since entirely freed myself of the impression that this life is a segment of existence which is enacted in a three-dimensional boxlike universe especially set up for it' (Jung 1967: 326). 'Our conscious world [is] a kind of illusion, (1967: 356). As Schopenhauer also said, 'We shall have a permanent notion or presentiment that under this reality in which we live and are there also lies concealed a second and different reality; it is the thing-in-itself, the *hupar* (the real in the proper sense) to this *onar* (our present life-dream)' (cited by Saher 1970: 68).

The first step in our return from exile is simply, not to complain (see *Consolatio* 1. 5. 6 ff.), but to hold fast to God's presence in us. That presence is happiness—not as if 'the substance of the happiness possessed is different from God the possessor' (*Consolatio* 3. 10. 46). Happiness, goodness, unity, and God are one and the same. 'Eternity is the whole, simultaneous and perfect possession of boundless life' (*Consolatio* 5. 6. 9). That is the life, half-glimpsed now from the shadows, that is the abiding reality of which our worlds are the stained reflections—and that is another story.

---

[2] James cites Ackerman at 1960: 78, but not with this gloss. I have not been able to track down the reference, miscopied into my notebook several years ago.

References

ABBOT, F. E. (1885), *Scientific Theism* (Macmillan: London).

ARMSTRONG, A. H. (1970), 'Plotinus': *Cambridge History of Later Greek and Early Mediaeval Philosophy*, ed. A. H. Armstrong (Cambridge University Press: Cambridge), 195–271.

AUDEN, W. H. (1966), *Collected Shorter Poems* (Faber: London).

AUGUSTINE (1923), *Confessions*, tr. T. Matthew, ed. R. Huddleston (Burns & Oates: London).

AUSTIN, R. W. J. (1980), 'Introduction': Ibn Arabi 1980, 1–44.

BARFIELD, O. (1965), *Saving the Appearances* (Harcourt, Brace & World: New York).

BECKER, E. (1973), *The Denial of Death* (Free Press: Glencoe, Ill.)

BENDER, T. K. (1966), *Gerard Manley Hopkins: The Classical Background and Critical Reception of his Work* (Johns Hopkins: Baltimore).

BERKELEY, G. (1948), *Collected Works*, ed. A. A. Luce and T. E. Jessop (Thomas Nelson: Edinburgh).

BERNARD, C. (1949), *Introduction to the Study of Experimental Medicine*, tr. H. C. Greene (Macmillan: New York).

BEVERIDGE, W. I. B. (1953), *The Art of Scientific Investigation* (Heinemann: London, 2nd edn.).

BLAKE, W. (1966), *Complete Writings*, ed. G. Keynes (Oxford University Press: London).

BLISH, J. (1967), *Black Easter* (Faber: London).

BOLER, J. F. (1963), *Charles Pierce and Scholastic Realism* (University of Washington Press: Seattle).

BORGES, J. L. (1964), *Other Inquisitions*, tr. R. L. C. Simms (University of Texas Press: Austin).

BOSWELL, J. (1953), *Life of Samuel Johnson* (Clarendon Press: Oxford).

BROWN, N. O. (1968), *Life against Death: The Psychoanalytic Meaning of History* (Sphere: London; 1st edn. RKP: 1959).

CALVINO, I. (1969), *Cosmicomics*, tr. W. Weaver (Cape: London).

CARDENAL, E. (1974), *Love*, tr. D. Livingstone (Search Press: London).

CARRITHERS, M., COLLINS, S., and LUKES, S. (eds.), (1985) *The Category of the Person* (Cambridge University Press: Cambridge).

CHERRY, C. (1980), *Nature and Religious Imagination* (Fortress Press: Philadelphia).

CHURCHLAND, P. (1984), *Matter and Consciousness* (MIT: Cambridge, Mass.).

CLARK, S. R. L. (1983), *Aristotle's Man* (Clarendon Press: Oxford; 2nd edn.)

CLARK, S. R. L. (1984), *From Athens to Jerusalem* (Clarendon Press: Oxford).

—— (1986*a*) 'Abstraction, Possession, Incarnation', in A. Kee and E. T. Long (eds.), *Being and Truth* (SCM: London), 293–317.

—— (1986*b*), *The Mysteries of Religion* (Blackwell: Oxford).

—— (1987), 'Animals, Ecosystems and the Liberal Ethic', *Monist*, 70: 114–33.

—— (1988*a*), 'Abstract Morality, Concrete Cases', in J. D. G. Evans (ed.), *Moral Philosophy and Contemporary Moral Philosophy* (Cambridge University Press: Cambridge), 35–54.

—— (1988*b*), 'Cupitt and Divine Imagining', *Modern Theology*, 5: 46–60.

—— (1988*c*), 'Is Humanity a Natural Kind?', in T. Ingold (ed.), *What is an Animal?* (Unwin Hyman: London), 17–34.

—— (1989*a*), 'Children and the Mammalian Order', in G. Scarre (ed.), *Children, Parents and Politics* (Cambridge University Press: Cambridge).

—— (1989*b*) *Civil Peace and Sacred Order* (Clarendon Press: Oxford).

—— (1990*a*), 'Reason as *Daimon*', in C. Gill (ed.), *The Person and the Human Mind* (Clarendon Press: Oxford, 187–206.

—— (1990*b*), 'Good Ethology and the Decent Polis', in H. Lesser and A. Loizou (eds.), *The Good of Community* (Gower Press: Epping).

COLE, T. (1967), *Democritus and the Sources of Greek Anthropology* (APA 15: Western Reserve University).

COTTER, J. F. (1972), *Inscape: The Christology and Poetry of Hopkins* (University of Pittsburgh Press: Pittsburgh).

CRANACH, M. VON (1979), 'Social Relations and Intergroup Conflict', in M. von Cranach, K. Foppa, W. Lepenies, D. Ploog (eds.), *Human Ecology* (Blackwells: Oxford), 423–8.

CUPITT, D. (1971), *Christ and the Hiddenness of God* (Lutterworth Press: London).

D'ARCY THOMPSON, W. (1917), *On Growth and Form* (Cambridge University Press: Cambridge).

DENNETT, D. C. (1978), *Brainstorms* (Harvester: Brighton).

DETIENNE, M. and VERNANT, J. P. (1978), *Cunning Intelligence in Greek Culture and Society* (Harvester: Brighton).

DE VOGEL, C. J. (1981), 'The Soma-Sema Formula', in H. J. Blumenthal and R. A. Markus (eds.), *Neoplatonism and Early Christian Thought* (Variorum: London).

DIHLE, A. (1982), *The Theory of Will in Classical Antiquity* (University of California Press: Berkeley).

DIONYSIUS (1971), *Writings of ps-Dionysius*, tr. C. E. Rolt (Paulist Press: New York).

Dodds, E. R. (1951), *The Greeks and the Irrational* (University of California Press: Berkeley).

—— (1968), *Pagan and Christian in an Age of Anxiety* (Cambridge University Press: Cambridge).

Donagan, A. (1977), *The Theory of Morality* (University of Chicago Press: Chicago).

Donne, J. (1929), *Complete Verse and Select Prose*, ed. J. Hayward (Nonesuch Press: London).

Drury, M. O'C. (1973), *The Danger of Words* (RKP: London).

Duerr, H. P. (1985), *Dreamtime: Concerning the Boundary between Wildness and Civilization*, tr. F. D. Goodman (Blackwells: Oxford).

Dunn, J. D. G. (1980), *Christology in the Making* (SCM Press: London).

Duns Scotus (1962), *Philosophical Writings*, tr. and ed. A. B. Wolter (Edinburgh University Press: Edinburgh).

Eller, V. (1973), *King Jesus' Manual of Arms for the 'Armless* (Abingdon Press: Nashville).

Elvin, M. (1985), 'Between the Earth and Heaven: Conceptions of the Self in China', in Carrithers *et al.* 1985: 156–90.

Evans-Pritchard, E. E. (1962), *Essays in Social Anthropology* (Faber: London).

Fawcett, D. (1916), *The World as Imagination* (Macmillan: London).

—— (1921), *Divine Imagining* (Macmillan: London).

Findlay, J. N. (1963), *Language, Mind and Value* (Allen and Unwin: London).

Foster, M. (1957), *Mystery and Philosophy* (SCM: London).

Fromm, E. (1974), *The Anatomy of Human Destructiveness* (Cape: London).

Frye, N. (1947), *Fearful Symmetry: A Study of William Blake* (Princeton University Press: Princeton).

Gadamer, H.-G. (1986). *The Idea of the Good in Platonic-Aristotelian Philosophy*, tr. P. C. Smith (Yale University Press: New Haven and London).

Gardner, H. (ed.) (1972), *New Oxford Book of English Verse* (Clarendon Press: Oxford).

Geach, P. (1969), *God and the Soul* (Routledge & Kegan Paul: London).

Goddard, D. (ed.) (1970), *A Buddhist Bible* (Beacon Press: Boston, Mass.).

Graves, R. (1966), *Poems* (Penguin: Harmondsworth).

Harner, M. (1982), *The Way of the Shaman* (Bantam: New York; 1st edn. 1980).

Harré, R. (1984), *Personal Being* (Harvard University Press: Boston, Mass.).

HAYWARD, J. W. (1987), *Shifting Worlds, Changing Minds* (Shambhala: Boston, Mass., and London).

HEAD, J. and CRANSTON, S. (eds.) (1977), *Reincarnation: The Phoenix Fire Mystery* (Julian Press: New York).

HEARNE, V. (1986), *Adam's Task* (A. A. Knopf: New York).

HEIDEGGER, M. (1968), *What is called Thinking?*, tr. F. D. Wieck and J. Glenn Gray (Harper and Row: New York).

HILLMAN, J. (1967), *Insearch: Psychology and Religion* (Hodder and Stoughton: London).

—— (1975), *Re-Visioning Psychology* (Harper & Row: New York).

—— (1983), *Archetypal Psychology* (Spring Books: Dallas).

HOLMES, S. (1984), *Benjamin Constant and the Making of Modern Liberalism* (Yale University Press: New Haven).

HOPKINS, G. M. (1959a), *Sermons and Other Devotional Writings*, ed. C. Devlin (Oxford University Press: Oxford).

—— (1959b), *Journals and Papers*, eds. H. House and G. Storey (Oxford University Press: Oxford).

—— (1970), *Poems*, ed. W. H. Gardner and N. H. Mackenzie (Oxford University Press: London).

HUME, D. (1888), *Treatise of Human Nature*, ed. L. A. Selby-Bigge (Clarendon Press: Oxford).

—— (1976), *Natural History of Religion and Dialogues Concerning Natural Religion*, ed. A. W. Colver and J. V. Price (Clarendon Press: Oxford).

IBN ARABI (1980), *The Bezels of Wisdom*, tr. R. W. J. Austin (Paulist Press: New York).

JAMES, W. (1897), *The Will to Believe* (Longmans, Green & Co: New York).

—— (1890), *Principles of Psychology* (Macmillan: London).

—— (1960), *The Varieties of Religious Experience* (Fontana: London; 1st published 1902).

JAYNES, J. (1976), *The Origin of Consciousness in the Breakdown of the Bicameral Mind* (Houghton Mifflin: New York).

JUNG, C. G. (1967), *Memories, Dreams, Reflections*, ed. A. Jaffe, tr. R. and A. C. Winston (Fontana: London).

KANT, I. (1930), *Lectures on Ethics* (Methuen: London).

—— (1953), *Prolegomena*, tr. P. G. Lewis (Manchester University Press: Manchester).

—— (1970), *Kant's Political Writings*, ed. H. Reiss (Cambridge University Press: Cambridge).

KING-FARLOW, J. (1978), *Self-Knowledge and Social Relations* (Science-History Publications: New York).

KIPLING, R. (1927), *Collected Verse 1885–1926* (Hodder & Stoughton: London).

KLEIN, D. B., (1951), *Abnormal Psychology* (Holt & Co.: New York.

KOYRE, A. (1968), *Metaphysics and Measurement* (Chapman & Hall: London).

LACY, A. (1967), *Miguel de Unamuno: The Rhetoric of Existence* (Mouton & Co.; The Hague).

LAMBERTON, R. (1986), *Homer the Theologian* (University of California Press: Berkeley).

LEGUIN, U. (1968), *A Wizard of Earthsea* (Gollancz: London).

LESSING, D. (1982), *The Making of the Representative of Planet 8* (Cape: London).

LEWIS, C. S. (1938), *Out of the Silent Planet* (John Lane: London).

—— (1955), *The Screwtape Letters* (Fontana: London 1955; 1st published 1942).

—— (1966), *Of Other Worlds* (Bles: London).

LIENHARDT, G. (1985), 'Self: Public, Private. Some African Representations', in Carrithers *et al.* 1985: 141–55.

LOCKE, J. (1963), *Two Treatises of Government*, ed. P. Laslett (Cambridge University Press: Cambridge).

LUTOSLAWSKI, W. (1924), *The World of Souls* (Allen & Unwin: London).

MCCARTHY, P. (1982), *Olaf Stapledon* (Twayne: Boston, Mass.).

MACINTYRE, A. (1981), *After Virtue* (Duckworth: London).

MACKIE, J. L. (1976), *Ethics: Inventing Right and Wrong* (Pelican: Harmondsworth).

MADELL, G. (1981), *The Identity of the Self* (Edinburgh University Press: Edinburgh).

MARCEL, G. (1951), *The Mystery of Being* (Harvill Press: London).

MARTIN, G. D. (1981), *The Architecture of Experience* (Edinburgh University Press: Edinburgh).

MATTHEWS, C. and J. (1985), *The Western Way* (Arkana: London).

MAUSS, M. (1985), 'A Category of the Human Mind', tr. W. D. Halls, in Carrithers *et al.* 1985: 1–25 (1st published 1938).

MAY, R. (1970), 'Psychotherapy and the demonic', in J. Campbell (ed.), *Myths, Dreams and Religion* (Dutton & Co.; New York), 196–210.

MERLAN, P. (1963), *Monopsychism, Mysticism, Metaconsciousness* (Nijhoff: The Hague).

MIDGLEY, M. (1984), *Wickedness* (Routledge & Kegan Paul: London).

MOORE, S. (1944), 'Gerard Manley Hopkins', *Downside Review*, 62: 184–95.

MONOD, J. (1972), *Chance and Necessity*, tr. A. Wainhouse (Collins: London).

Morris, T. V. (1986), *The Logic of God Incarnate* (Cornell University Press: Ithaca and London).

Murdoch, I. (1987), *The Brotherhood of the Book* (Chatto & Windus: London).

Nance, J. (1986), *The Gentle Tasaday* (Godine: Boston, Mass., pbk).

Nash, R. H. (1969), *The Light of the Mind* (University Press of Kentucky: Lexington).

Newman, J. H. (1979), *An Essay Concerning the Grammar of Assent* (Notre Dame Press: Notre Dame; 1st published 1870).

Nilsson, M. P. (1949), 'Letter to Professor A. D. Nock on Some Fundamental Concepts in the Science of Religion', *Harvard Theological Review*, 42: 79–110.

Nitzsche, J. C. (1975), *The Genius Figure in Antiquity and the Middle Ages* (Columbia University Press: New York).

O'Daly, G. (1973), *Plotinus' Philosophy of the Self* (Irish University Press: Shannon).

Ornstein, R. (1986), *Multimind* (Houghton Mifflin: New York).

Pannenberg, W. (1969), *Theology and the Kingdom of God*, ed. R. J. Neuhaus (Westminster Press: Philadelphia).

Peirce, C. S. (1934), *Collected Papers*, ed. C. Hartshorne and P. Weiss (Harvard University Press: Cambridge, Mass.).

Penfield, W. (1975), *The Mystery of the Mind* (Princeton University Press: Princeton).

Perry, T. D. (1976), *Moral Reasoning and Truth* (Clarendon Press: Oxford).

Philo of Alexandria (1929), *Collected Works*, vols. i-xi, tr. F. H. Colson, G. H. Whitaker, *et al.*, Loeb Classical Library (Heinemann: London).

Philokalia (1979) ed. G. E. H. Palmer, P. Sherrard, and K. Ware, vol. i (Faber: London).

Pieper, J. (1952), *Leisure the Basis of Culture*, tr. R. and C. Winston (Faber: London).

—— (1965), *Love and Inspiration*, tr. R. and C. Winston (Faber: London).

—— (1969), *Death and Immortality*, tr. R. and C. Winston (Burns & Oates: London).

Plotinus (1978–88), *Enneads*, tr. A. H. Armstrong, Loeb Classical Library (Heinemann: London).

Polya, G. (1954), *Patterns of Plausible Inference* (Oxford University Press: London).

Potts, T. C. (1980), *Conscience in Medieval Philosophy* (Cambridge University Press: Cambridge).

Puccetti, R. (1975), 'Is Pain Necessary?', *Philosophy*, 50: 259–70.

RADCLIFFE-BROWN, A. R. (1940), *Structure and Function in Society* Cohen & West: London).

RAHULA, W. (1978), *Zen and the Taming of the Bull* (Gordon Fraser: London).

RAINE, K. (1956), *Collected Poems* (Hamilton: London).

—— (1982), *The Inner Journey of the Poet* (Allen & Unwin: London).

ROBINSON, T. M. (1970), *Plato's Psychology* (University of Toronto Press: Toronto).

SAHER, P. J. (1970), *Happiness and Immortality* (Allen & Unwin: London).

SAID, E. (1978), *Orientalism* (Random House Inc.: New York).

SANDEL, M. J. (1982) *Liberalism and the Limits of Justice* (Cambridge University Press: Cambridge).

SANDERS, E. P. (1971), *The Family* (Hunt-Davis: London).

SATPREM (1968) *Sri Aurobindo: The Adventure of Consciousness*, tr. Tehmi (Aurobindo Ashram: Pondicherry).

SCHELL, J. (1982), *The Fate of the Earth* (Pan Books: London).

SEXTUS EMPIRICUS (1933), *Works*, tr. R. G. Bury, Loeb Classical Library (Heinemann: London).

SHEA, W. R. (1972), *Galileo's Intellectual Revolution* (Macmillan: London).

SINGER, J. (1973), *Boundaries of the Soul* (Gollancz: London).

SNELL, B. (1953), *The Discovery of the Mind*, tr. R. G. Rosenmeyer (Dover: New York).

SOLOVYEV, V. (1948), *Lectures on Godmanhood*, ed. P. P. Zouboff (Dennis Dobson Ltd.: London).

SPENGLER, O. (1926), *The Decline of the West*, tr. C. F. Atkinson (Knopf: New York).

SPINOZA, B. (1982), *Ethics*, tr. S. Shirley, ed. S. Feldman (Hackett: Indianapolis).

SPRIGGE, T. (1983), *The Vindication of Absolute Idealism* (Edinburgh University Press: Edinburgh).

STAPLEDON, O. (1935), *Odd John* (Methuen: London).

—— (1937), *Star Maker* (Methuen: London).

—— (1946), *Death into Life* (Methuen: London).

—— (1947), *The Flames* (Secker & Warburg: London).

—— (1954), *The Opening of the Eyes* (Methuen: London).

—— (1963), *Last and First Men* (Penguin: Harmonsworth; 1st published 1930).

TERESA OF AVILA 1961, *Interior Castle* tr. E. Allison Peers (Doubleday: New York; 1st published 1944).

THOREAU, W. D. (1910), *Walden* (J. M. Dent: London).

TUAN, YI-FU (1974), *Topophilia* (Prentice-Hall: Englewood Cliffs).

VENDLER, Z. (1985), *The Matter of Minds* (Clarendon Press: Oxford).

VERDENIUS, V. J. (1942), *Parmenides* (Wodters: Groningen).

VERNANT, J. P. (1983), *Myth and Thought among the Greeks* (Routledge & Kegan Paul: London).

—— and VIDAL-NAQUET, P. (1981), *Tragedy and Myth in Ancient Greece*, tr. J. Lloyd (Harvester Press: Brighton).

VICKERS, B. (1984), 'Analogy versus Identity', in B. Vickers (ed.), *Occult and Scientific Mentalities in the Renaissance* (Cambridge University Press: Cambridge), 95–163.

VYCINAS, V. (1972), *Search for Gods* (Nijhoff: The Hague).

WALEY, A. (1935), 'Introduction' to Murasaki Shikibu, *The Tale of Genji*, tr. A. Waley (Allen & Unwin: London), vii–xvi.

WALKER, D. (1958), *Spiritual and Demonic Magic from Ficino to Campanella* (Warburg Institute: London).

WALKER, R. C. S. (1985), 'Idealism: Kant and Berkeley', in J. Foster and H. M. Robinson (eds.), *Essays on Berkeley* (Clarendon Press: Oxford), 109–30.

WALLAS, G. (1926), *The Art of Thought* (Harcourt, Brace: New York).

WALLIS, R. T. (1972), *Neo-Platonism* (Duckworth: London).

WARREN, E. W. (1964), 'Consciousness in Plotinus', *Phronesis*, 9: 83–97.

WEAVER, R. M. (1987), *Southern Essays*, ed. G. M. Curtis (Liberty Press: Indianapolis).

WEIL, S. (1956), *Notebooks*, tr. A. F. Wills (Routledge & Kegan Paul: London).

—— (1978), *Lectures on Philosophy* (Cambridge University Press: Cambridge).

—— (1987), *The Need for Roots*, tr. A. F. Wills (Routledge & Kegan Paul; 1st published 1952).

WHITE, V. (1985), *The Fall of a Sparrow* (Paternoster Press: Exeter).

WINK, W. (1986), *Unmasking the Powers* (Fortress Press: Philadelphia).

WITTGENSTEIN, L. (1961), *Tractatus Logico-Philosophicus*, tr. D. F. Pears and B. F. McGuinness (Routledge & Kegan Paul: London).

YEATS, W. B. (1950), *Poems* (Macmillan: London).

—— (1955), *Autobiographies* (Macmillan: London).

—— (1961), *Essays and Introductions* (Macmillan: London).

ZAEHNER, R. C. (1974), *Our Savage God* (Collins: London).

ZIMMER, H. (1967), *Philosophies of India*, ed. J. Campbell (Routledge & Kegan Paul: London, 2nd edn.).

ZIZIOULAS, J. (1985), *Being as Communion* (Darton, Longman & Todd: London).

Index